A GARDENER'S GUIDE TO

ANNUALS

A magnificent selection of annuals and biennials
for a superb display of colour in the garden

Venidium fastuosum

Tagetes erecta 'Orange Jubilee' F1

A GARDENER'S GUIDE TO

ANNUALS

A magnificent selection of annuals and biennials for a superb display of colour in the garden

BOB LEGGE

Published by Salamander Books Limited
LONDON

A Salamander Book

Published by Salamander Books Ltd.
52 Bedford Row,
London WC1R 4LR.

ISBN 0 86101 412 X

Distributed by
Hodder and Stoughton Services,
PO Box 6, Mill Road, Dunton Green,
Sevenoaks, Kent TN13 2XX.

Contents

Text and colour photographs are cross-referenced throughout as follows: 64▶. The plants are arranged in alphabetical order of Latin name. Page numbers in **bold** refer to text entries; those in *italics* refer to photographs.

Credits

Author: Until his recent death, Bob Legge was Superintendent of the Central Royal Parks, London. His career in horticulture spanned over 30 years, from training at Bicton and the RHS Garden at Wisley to radio and TV broadcasts. He was a member of the RHS Floral Committee and regularly exhibited at the Chelsea Flower Show. This book communicates his enthusiasm for growing plants and serves as a tribute to his dedication and skill.

Consultant: Ralph Gould has spent over 50 years in horticulture, specializing in raising new flower strains.
Editor: Geoff Rogers
Designer: Roger Hyde
Colour and monochrome reproductions: Bantam Litho Ltd., England.
Filmset: SX Composing Ltd., England.
Printed in Belgium by
Henri Proost & Cie, Turnhout.

Introduction

Over many years, careful and methodical selection by plant breeders has enabled gardeners to grow a very wide range of annual, biennial and perennial plants with greater ease than in the past. The frustration of having to wait an age for a plant to flower has be dispelled; most of the varieties included here will bloom in the same season. Other species, which may be biennals or perennials in the wild, will usually flower or produce their decorative foliage within the year, if they are sown early enough, in the same manner as true annuals.

Generally easy to grow, most of them can be used to good effect around the garden and home. There is an excellent variety of containers for yards and patios, and window boxes and hanging baskets may be planted to fill small corners.

Annuals can fill bare gaps that appear after early-flowering subjects, such as bulbs and perennials, have finished flowering. Many kinds can be sown at intervals to give a succession of blooms.

F1 hybrids

In recent years much research has gone into the production of many new F1 hybrid flowers. Gardeners now enjoy a much wider choice of variety than ever before. Although the seed of F1 hybrids is generally more expensive than that of older kinds, their advantages in colour, flower size, plant habit and general performance are well worth the extra cost of the seed.

In some cases these improvements are retained in part in the second generation, called F2 hybrids, which are usually cheaper, but still better than ordinary strains.

These hybrids result from first and second generation crosses

Left: **Lavatera trimestris**
This elegant species brings colour to the garden in midsummer. The blooms are 10cm (4in) across and borne on stems up to 1m (39in) tall. Lovely varieties are available.

Below: **Brassica oleracea acephala**
Ornamental cabbages can be used to great effect as spot plants near the front of the border. Sow the seeds in spring and check for caterpillars.

Above:
Tagetes patula 'Yellow Jacket'
A beautifully compact French marigold ideal for edging a border.

Right:
Tropaeolum majus 'Whirlybird'
This colourful nasturtium variety will thrive on the poorest of soils.

made between two parent lines specially bred and selected for their ability to produce the desirable qualities that the breeder has in mind, and which go to make a good garden plant. In some instances, such as petunias, the introduction of F1 hybrids has almost completely superseded the older cultivars within the space of a few years. The range of species that are bred by this method is gradually extending to enrich further our homes and gardens.

Propagation

All the kinds listed in the guide are grown from seed. Many of these will not require a greenhouse or frame but can be sown directly where they are to flower. In fact a number of annuals with small roots or tap-rooted systems do not transplant readily and can best be sown where they are to flower when soil conditions are suitable. Some species that have seeds large enough to handle may be sown direct into small peat pots or other containers; this avoids both pricking off and the risk of root disturbance that may occur when transplanting seedlings.

When seedlings are being pricked off or transplanted into trays from the containers in which the seed was broadcast, they are best planted with sufficient space to allow development of the planting-out stage. Thin sowings enable this task to be carried out as early as possible, before much root development has taken place.

Outdoor sowings may be either broadcast in patches or put into shallow drills or grooves drawn at intervals to allow for the full development of plants. The drills should be drawn in different directions if more than one kind of seed is sown in a border, so that the groups or patches will look less formal. In both cases the seed should be only lightly covered with fine soil.

Drills will be easier to thin and weed, particularly when seedling weeds are likely to be troublesome. Thinning should be gradual and done in stages as seedlings develop. On some soils, if difficulty is experienced in making a good seed bed, it may be an advantage to cover seeds with some moistened peat.

As noted under certain species that are hardy, there is usually much to be gained, in strength and in earlier flowering, if plants are sown in the autumn. In the event of a severe winter killing them, this does give another opportunity to sow in the spring.

Many hardy annuals are admirable for filling in bare places in the garden after early spring flowering bulbs and plants are finished. Direct sowings usually start in early spring, as soon as the soil is suitably dry and crumbly.

Position

Because many species need to complete their growth in one season it is essential to give them the most suitable position possible and to allow room for their full development. A sunny site will suit most but many will tolerate partial shade and a few full shade.

Since heights vary, the taller varieties are best planted towards the back of one-sided borders, or centrally in a more formal area or where the plants may be viewed from various aspects. Those plants of intermediate height should be grown nearer the front, and the shortest or most compact kinds are the most suitable for edging.

Annual climbers may effectively be used as a background, on trellis or wire mesh, or even as groups grown wigwam fashion; there are many excellent kinds of plastic mesh suited to this purpose. Some kinds of climbers could be used to scramble over a hedge, or old tree stumps, or a bank where little else will grow. The tall climbing nasturtiums, for example, are very effective when used in this way.

Culture

Failures in all stages of development, from seedling through to flowering, can often be attributed to such causes as over- or under-watering, or seeds may have been sown too deeply or in unsuitable temperatures; pests and diseases can also take their toll if precautions are not observed.

Keep the soil just moist throughout their growing life and if possible water seedlings early in the day so that they do not remain wet overnight, which encourages the growth of diseases such as those causing damping-off and root rots.

Watering from above in full sunshine may result in leaf scorch, and drying-out of seeds during germination may kill them. Some shading at this stage is usually beneficial but should be removed before seedlings become drawn or elongated.

A number of excellent seed and growing-on mediums are now readily obtainable, and suitable for growing most kinds of annuals.

The use of suitable greenhouse sprays and smokes as soon as any pests or diseases are observed should ensure healthy plants.

The recommendations for thin sowing, whether indoors or out, must be noted; overcrowded and starved seedlings rarely develop into vigorous plants, and in any case are usually difficult to handle.

Hardening off

This stage of a seedling's life may be critical if sudden changes of temperature occur. Those plants raised in heat and intended for outdoor planting need to be gradually accustomed to lower temperatures and more airy conditions a week or two before planting out. This will depend on the species and the locality.

Tender or half-hardy kinds should be protected from frost or cold winds until very late spring. A short period during which plants stand in a sheltered position outdoors will help the hardening-off process and avoid any check in growth that might occur.

Planting out

The planting area should be prepared well beforehand, working in any necessary addition of compost or fertilizer. Seedlings should be watered a few hours before planting out and also afterwards if the soil is dry. Spacing must be sufficient to allow the full development of the species. Of course, cultivation and weeding should be carried out at suitable intervals.

Remove dead flowerheads where possible, to promote continued flowering, and destroy any plants that become affected by disease.

Above:
Eschscholzia 'Harlequin Hybrids'
A stunning variety of the Californian poppy that will revel in a sunny and dry location. Flowers all summer.

Left:
Begonia semperflorens 'Venus'
A compact cultivar of fibrous-rooted begonia with relatively large deep rose flowers. Grow in light moist soil.

Above: **Alonsoa warscewiczii**
Slender stems of dainty scarlet flowers appear in succession for many weeks in the summer. 18▸

Below: **Ageratum houstonianum 'Adriatic Blue' F1**
Neat cushions of fluffy blue flowers for carpeting and border edgings. 17▸

Above: **Althaea rosea**
The showy upstanding hollyhocks put on a splendid show in summer. They look especially effective when planted against a wall. Avoid windy areas or stake plants. 18▸

Above: **Amaranthus caudatus**
This vigorous plant produces lovely crimson tassels during midsummer. Grow them in groups in a mixed border or singly in containers. The leaves bronze with age. 19▸

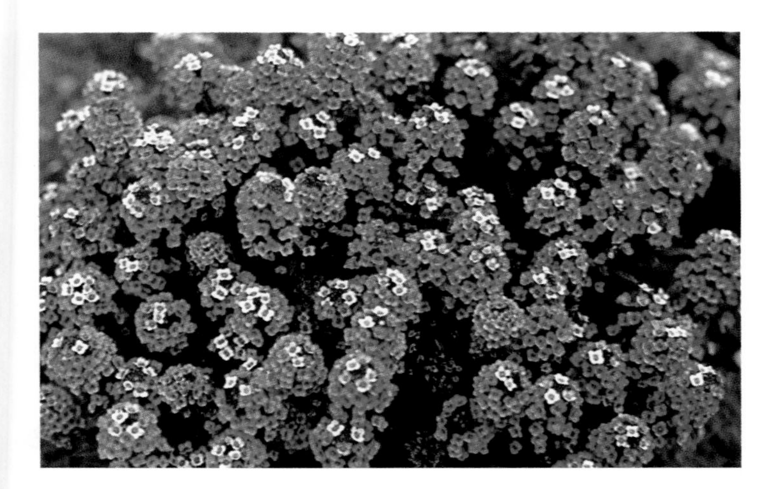

Above: **Alyssum maritimum 'Violet Queen'**
These scented plants are ideal for ground cover and edgings. 19▸

Below: **Angelica archangelica**
A double bonus of aromatic feathery foliage and greenish yellow flowers. Striking as an architectural plant. 21▸

Above:
Antirrhinum 'Trumpet Serenade'
An unusual, tubular-flowered mixture of bicoloured blooms. 22▸

Below: **Argemone mexicana**
Large, light golden blooms appear against spiny, silvery green leaves. Grow in a light soil in the sun. 23▸

Adonis aestivalis

(Pheasant's eye)

- **Sow in spring**
- **Ordinary soil, with added peat**
- **Partly shaded or sunny position**

This hardy annual is of outstanding beauty; the deep crimson petals of the flower contrast vividly with the near-black stamens in the centre of the cup-shaped flowers. Growing on stems 30cm (12in) high, the leaves are fine, deeply cut, and almost fern-like. It is a beautiful plant for all.

Sow seed in any good growing medium in spring, prick off and grow on in the usual way. Plant out into final positions in late spring at 30cm (12in) apart. Alternatively sow seeds where they are to flower in the autumn. Once germinated make the first thinning at 15cm (6in) spacings. The following early spring complete spacing to 30cm (12in). Germination may be slow, so be patient.

Ideally suited to the front of a border, they combine very well with other annuals and biennials. When designing an area for these plants make sure you plan for bold drifts to get maximum effect. They can also be used in containers.

Take care

Watch for slug damage.

Ageratum houstonianum

- **Sow in spring**
- **Most ordinary types of soil**
- **Tolerates all positions except heavy shade**

Flowering from early summer onwards these beautiful plants resemble small powder puffs from a distance. Shown to their best when edging a formal bedding scheme, they are also good subjects for window boxes and containers.

Try to use the F1 hybrids now available; these give larger and longer trusses of blooms. The cultivar 'Adriatic' is in this class: its height is 20cm (8in), and the mid-blue flower is produced above light green hairy leaves. Although most cultivars are in the blue range there are a few whites now available.

Sow seed in boxes of growing medium in spring, under glass. When large enough to handle, prick out in the usual way. Plant out in final positions at the end of spring or when the risk of frost has disappeared. Until planting out try to maintain a temperature of 10-16°C (50-60°F); lower than this will tend to check the growth of young plants.

Take care

Avoid planting out too early. 12▸

Alonsoa warscewiczi

(Mask flower)

- **Sow in late winter or early spring**
- **Rich and well-drained soil**
- **Sunny location**

Introduced from Peru this splendid plant grows to a height of 30-60cm (12-24in). Striking saucer-shaped red flowers are produced on reddish branched stems from summer to late autumn, 2-3cm (0.8-1.25in) in diameter. Leaves are ovate and a rich dark green.

Annual in habit, it requires a heated greenhouse for propagation; a temperature of 16°C (60°F), maintained up to planting-out time, will suffice. Sow the seeds in pots of a good growing medium in late winter or early spring. Prick out into boxes or individual pots when the seedlings are large enough. Grow on in gentle heat until late spring. Harden off in the usual way and plant out into permanent positions, approximately 30-40cm (12-15in) apart. Choose a sunny position for the best results and make sure the soil is free-draining, otherwise flowers will be disappointing. Stake with bushy twigs if necessary.

Take care

Do not overwater. 12▸

Althaea rosea

(Hollyhock)

- **Sow in spring**
- **Heavy and rich soil**
- **Sheltered position but not shade**

Hollyhocks are probably the tallest plants you are likely to deal with in an ordinary garden. There are many varieties to choose from but *A. rosea* and its cultivars are by far the easiest. Flowers are produced on short stalks directly from the main stem; they range in colour from pink and red to white and light yellow. Up to 10cm (4in) in diameter, they can be single or double.

Treat as a biennial to obtain the tallest plants, by sowing where they are to flower in early summer. Take out shallow drills 23cm (9in) apart. Thin out seedlings in summer to 60cm (24in) apart. Such plants will attain a height of 2.7m (9ft) the following summer.

For annual treatment, sow on site in spring in the same way, and thin out to 38cm (15in) apart. Plants treated in this way will flower in the same year, reaching a height of about 1.8m (6ft).

Take care

Mulch in spring, and water freely in dry weather. 13▸

Alyssum maritimum

(Lobularia maritima)

- **Sow in early spring**
- **Ordinary soil**
- **Full sun**

An annual of extraordinary resilience, mainly because of its ability to self-seed in great quantities. Some gardeners have difficulty in eradicating it from the garden. Mats of tiny flowers are produced on short stems 7.5-10cm (3-4in) from early summer onwards if plants are sown directly where they are to flower in spring.

Plants can be raised by sowing seeds in boxes of seed-growing medium a month earlier. Prick out the seedlings into a free-draining potting medium when large enough to handle. Plant out in final positions in mid-spring. To prolong the flowering period make a further sowing in late spring.

Commonly used for edging formal beds and borders, this species can also be used effectively with other annuals in window boxes and containers. Other colours include rose pink, mauve, purple and lilac.

Take care

Use slug bait in spring. 15▸

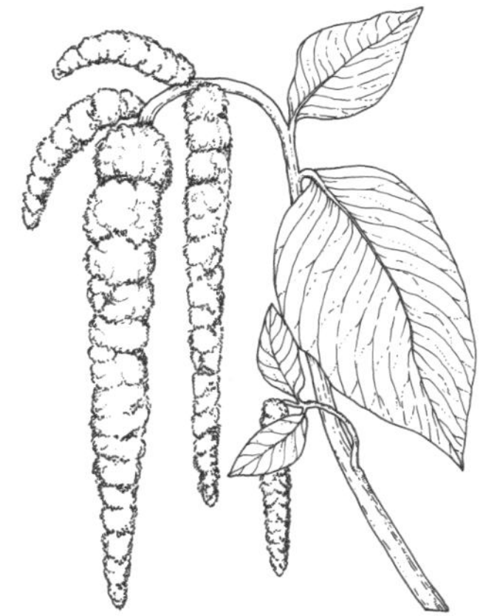

Amaranthus caudatus

(Love-lies-bleeding)

- **Sow in spring**
- **Well-cultivated soil**
- **Sunny location**

The long tail-like racemes of crimson flowers of this plant can reach 45cm (18in) in length. The flowers are produced on stems up to 105cm (3.5ft) tall. Leaves are ovate in shape and green in colour, the latter changing to bronze as the season progresses. *A. caudatus* is used mainly in formal beds as a 'spot' plant to give height. Try them as individual specimens in largish containers or in groups on a mixed border. The flowers appear in summer.

For borders sow the seed directly into the open ground in spring in a sunny position. When thinning out seedlings give plenty of room for development, about 60cm (24in) apart.

Raise plants for containers and formal borders by sowing in boxes of good seed-growing medium in early spring, prick off into individual pots under glass, and plant out into final positions in late spring.

Take care

Keep well watered in dry periods. 14▸

Anagallis caerulea

(Pimpernel)

- **Sow from spring onwards**
- **Ordinary well-drained soil**
- **Sunny location**

The hybrids and species related to the common scarlet pimpernel have now become many gardeners' favourites for planting in various parts of the garden. This beautiful blue species is low growing. Not much taller than 10cm (4in), the flowers are borne on semi-prostrate stems about 1.25cm (0.5in) in diameter and saucer-shaped. These appear from early summer onwards.

Easily grown on light soils, they can be directly sown where they are to flower. Take out shallow drills 1.25cm (0.5in) deep in spring, sow in the drills, and cover. Thin out the subsequent seedlings to 15cm (6in) apart. If soil conditions remain dry, water once a week until a good germination can be seen, then ease off the watering. Use near the edge of borders, containers and window boxes, and try a few plants in small pockets on the rock garden.

Take care

Do not overwater plants.

Anchusa capensis 'Blue Angel'

- **Sow in spring or autumn**
- **Ordinary well-drained soil**
- **Open sunny position**

This improved compact form of the wild tall species, originating from the Cape, grows only about 23cm (9in) high. The plants form neat clumps covered with ultramarine blue flowers for a considerable period. The many branching stems arise from a basal rosette of neat dark green leaves.

For early flowering, sow seed in heat in winter in seed mixture. Prick out seedlings in trays, or singly in small pots. They should be grown cool and hardened off ready for planting out in spring. Sow also outdoors in spring or in early autumn where they are to flower. Seedlings should finally be thinned to about 20cm (8in) apart. Remove dead blooms to encourage a further display. A few autumn-sown seedlings make an early indoor show if grown in 10cm (4in) pots in a cold greenhouse. Keep well watered in dry spells.

Take care

Spray against mildew in dry conditions.

Angelica archangelica

(Angelica)

- **Sow in spring**
- **Rich easily worked soil**
- **Partial shade**

A large hardy biennial, usually grown for two purposes: as a culinary herb for glazing, and as an architectural plant for the back of a large border. Umbels of yellow-green flowers open in summer; these are carried on thick hollow stems, 2-3m (6.5-10ft) in height. For the average garden three or four plants should be adequate to cover both purposes.

Sow the seed outdoors in mid-spring to flower the following year. Shallow drills deep enough to take the flat seed can be taken out in a spare part of the vegetable garden. Thin out seedlings to 30cm (12in). Plant out into final positions the following spring. Plants will die once seed has been set, but by keeping the flowers cut off a further useful year's growth can be obtained. Others left to seed will produce more than enough young plants for ordinary purposes in ensuing years. Stems should be cut young in early summer for culinary uses.

Take care

Give plants plenty of room. 15▶

Antirrhinum majus 'Guardsman'

(Snapdragon)

- **Sow late winter/early spring**
- **Light to medium soil**
- **Sunny position**

An intermediate antirrhinum of great merit, 'Guardsman' is brilliant scarlet with a white throat and yellow lips to the open parts of the central petals. Growing to a height of 38-45cm (15-18in) this cultivar is very free flowering.

As this is a half-hardy annual, sow seeds in late winter under glass or in early spring in a temperature of 16-18°C (60-65°F). Use a good peat-based growing medium or make up your own (without nutrients) of equal parts of peat and sand. Sow seed thinly and cover only lightly. Seedlings are prone to damping off disease and this is often caused by a too rich growing medium so beware. Prick off into boxes when large enough to handle. Harden off and plant out in early summer at 23cm (9in) apart.

Take care

Pinch out the central growing point when the young plants are 10cm (4in) high; this makes bushier plants.

Antirrhinum majus 'Trumpet Serenade'

(Snapdragon)

- **Sow in winter to spring**
- **Light to medium soil**
- **Sunny location**

Because of the introduction of rust-resistant cultivars the snapdragons have now returned to favour. There are many to choose from, either for planting in beds or borders or – the tall types – for use as cut flowers. The range of colours available makes it difficult to choose, but for ordinary garden purposes try the mixture 'Trumpet Serenade'. Having a dwarf bushy habit they are ideal for bedding out from the end of spring onwards. Trumpet-shaped flowers in red, pink, yellow and shades of orange are carried on 30cm (12in) stems. Leaves are a shiny dark green and ovate.

Sow seed on a peat-based growing medium in late winter or early spring, and lightly cover the seed. Keep in a temperature of 16-21°C (60-70°F). Prick off seedlings in the usual way, grow on until the end of spring, then gradually harden off.

Take care

Be sure to use a good quality medium for sowing seeds. 16▸

Antirrhinum nanum 'Floral Carpet'

(Snapdragon)

- **Sow late winter/early spring**
- **Light to medium soil**
- **Sunny site**

This is an excellent mixture of dwarf bushy uniform plants bearing many stems of bright blooms about 20cm (8in) high.

Sow from late winter to early spring in heat, or in late summer to overwinter under cold glass for earlier flowering. Sow seed very thinly in seed-growing mixture and germinate in a temperature of 16-18°C (60-65°F). Barely cover seed with mixture and shade from bright sun until germination. Prick out seedlings into trays and grow on in a lower temperature until ready to harden off. Antirrhinums may be planted out in late spring or early summer, about 23cm (9in) apart. The dwarf strains need no pinching out because they branch naturally. Remove dead flower spikes as soon as possible to prevent seed formation and encourage flowering.

Take care

Although antirrhinums are perennials best results are obtained from vigorous seedlings.

Arctotis × hybrida

(African daisy)

- **Sow in mid-spring**
- **Ordinary soil**
- **Sunny position**

Perennial in habit, this daisy is better treated as an annual for its very fine large blooms in the first year. Many plants can be lost through the winter months. Large flowers up to 10cm (4in) across can be produced from spring sowings, on stems up to 60cm (24in) tall. The narrow grey-green leaves are a lovely foil for the apricot, yellow, white or red blooms.

Choose the middle part of a sunny border to get the best from these plants. In spring make direct sowings where they are to flower. Rake the ground down to a fine tilth, take out drills 30cm (12in) apart, sow the seed thinly and cover. When germination is complete thin the seedlings in the drills to 30cm (12in) apart. Flowers will appear from early summer and keep blooming until the first frosts. As growth continues, use shortened peasticks around the plants to give a little support.

Take care

Keep plants well weeded in the early stages of growth.

Argemone mexicana

(Prickly poppy)

- **Sow in mid-spring**
- **Light and dry soil**
- **Sunny position**

This unusual annual, introduced from the semi- and tropical areas of America, is as the name implies prickly. Extremely majestic orange or yellow flowers will appear from early summer onwards and some protection is given to them by the prickly stems and leaves, the latter being pinnate and glaucous. Some individual flowers can be up to 9cm (3.5in) in diameter and being scented they will attract a number of flying insects. Reaching a height of 60cm (24in) the stems are straggly; do not however try to support them, or you will probably do more harm than good.

Sow seeds in boxes of ordinary seed-growing medium in spring at a temperature of 16°C (60°F), prick out into boxes in the usual way and plant into final positions at 30cm (12in) apart in late spring. Alternatively sow directly into the border in a sunny position during mid-spring, and later thin out to correct spacings.

Take care

Dead-head to prolong flowering 16◆

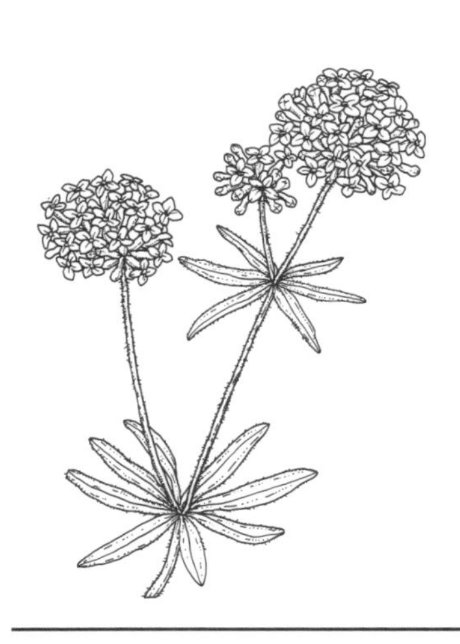

Asperula orientalis

(Annual woodruff)

- **Sow in mid-spring**
- **Ordinary but moist soil**
- **Partial shade**

The pale blue flowers of this semi-dwarf annual are strongly aromatic, and this species has a long flowering period. The tubular flowers are borne in bunches at the end of 30cm (12in) stems on which are whorls of narrow lanceolate hairy leaves.

Because of its ability to tolerate partial shade it can be used in some of the more difficult parts of the garden, and it is also valuable for ground cover purposes.

Sow in mid-spring on prepared ground where the plants are to flower. Rake the ground down to a fine tilth, broadcast the seed over the given area, and lightly rake in the seed. When germination has taken place thin out to 10cm (4in) apart.

For very early flowering in pots for the patio or windowsill, sow seed in the autumn; plant five or six seedlings to a 13cm (5in) pot, grow on through the winter in a cool position, and these will flower in spring.

Take care

Keep soil moist.

Begonia semperflorens

(Fibrous-rooted begonia)

- **Sow in late winter**
- **Light, slightly moist soil**
- **Semi-shade, or some sun**

Of all the summer annuals the begonia must rank high on the list of most gardeners. A very wide range of this group of plants is available: short, tall or medium in height, green or copper foliage, red, pink or white flowers. However they are tender and therefore some heat will be necessary at propagating time if good results are expected. Try a batch of the cultivar 'Venus'; this plant grows to a height of 15cm (6in) and has deep rose flowers large for its type. Plants spread to about 15cm (6in) across.

Sow seeds on a peat-based growing medium in late winter. Mix the seed with a little fine sand before sowing, to enable it to be sown more evenly. Do not cover the seed. Place in a temperature of 21°C (70°F). When they are large enough to handle, prick off the seedlings in the usual way. Plant out into final positions in early summer, after the danger of frost.

Take care

Do not plant out too early. 10▸

Borago officinalis

(Borage)

- **Sow in mid-spring**
- **Ordinary soil**
- **Sunny location**

This annual native herb is grown for its foliage and flowers and as a valuable addition to summer salads. Usually attaining a height of 1m (39in), the plants are better suited to the middle or back of a large border; group them together in fours or fives for a bold effect. Larger plants will need staking. The large leaves are obovate, tending to narrow at the base, covered with hairs (as are the long stems), and a good green in colour. Flowers are generally blue, but purple and white forms occur. About 2cm (0.8in) across, they resemble five-pointed stars.

This species is very easy to grow. Sow the seeds where the plants are to flower, in mid-spring. Take out small drills and cover the seed. Later thin them out to 30cm (12in) apart. Flowering begins in early summer.

Dried flowers of borage can be used to enhance the ever-popular pot-pourri; blooms are collected before they fully open.

Take care

Clear unwanted seedlings. 33▸

Brachycome iberidifolia

(Swan River daisy)

- **Sow in mid-spring**
- **Rich soil**
- **Sunny but sheltered site**

The daisy flowers of this half-hardy annual may be lilac, blue-purple, pink or white. Very free-flowering and fragrant, the blooms are produced on compact plants from early summer onwards. It is very striking when sited towards the front of a border, and can also be planted in containers on a sunny sheltered patio or yard. Wiry stems reach a height of 45cm (18in) and carry light green leaves that are deeply cut. The scented flowers, when fully open, are about 4cm (1.6in) across.

Sow the seed under glass in spring. Use a good ordinary seed-growing medium, and keep in a temperature of 16°C (60°F). When seedlings are ready, prick off in the usual way. Set plants out at 35cm (14in) intervals in late spring. Alternatively, sow seed directly into the border during mid-spring and thin out later. Some support may be necessary.

Take care

Avoid windy sites. 34▸

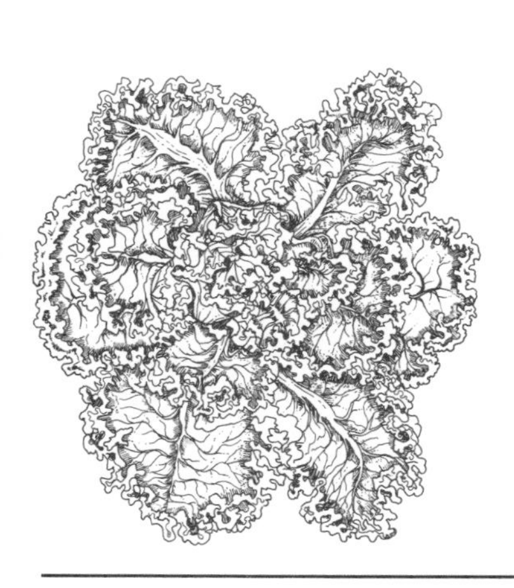

Brassica oleracea acephala

(Ornamental cabbage)

- **Sow in mid-spring**
- **Ordinary but not too acid soil**
- **Moist, not too shady position**

Grown with great panache by the Victorians, today's cultivars vary in size, shape and colour and can be safely planted with other annuals to add interest. Of the brassica (cabbage) family the two main types are the open Savoy cabbages and the somewhat taller kales. Colours range from pure white to pale yellow, pink, purple and light red. Use the Savoy types near the front of a border, and the kales towards the centre or back. The latter can be effective 'spot' plants.

Sow seed thinly in drills, in early spring. Cover the seed to a depth of 2cm (0.8in). When they are large enough plant the seedlings into permanent positions. Spacing will depend on the cultivar so read the growing instructions on the seed packet carefully. Remember that all brassicas are prone to various pests and diseases, but in particular pigeons, which can decimate them.

Take care

Spray against caterpillars in early summer. 7◆

Calandrinia umbellata

(Rock purslane)

- **Sow in spring**
- **Light, sandy soil**
- **Full sun, but sheltered site**

This dwarf plant, grown as an annual in milder areas or as a biennial elsewhere, is best suited to a sunny sheltered spot in the garden. As it grows to only 15cm (6in), put it in small pockets on the rock garden or at the front of a border. The crimson to purple flowers, 2cm (0.8in) across, are bowl-shaped, and open from early summer onwards. Mats of short stems carry linear, grey-green leaves.

For annual propagation sow seed under glass in spring in any good seed-growing medium; keep in a temperature of 16°C (60°F), prick out in the usual way, and grow on at a temperature of 10-16°C (50-60°F). Harden off and plant out in late spring at 23-30cm (9-12in) intervals.

As a biennial sow the seed during early summer where the plants are to flower the following year. Thin out the seedlings before the end of the summer, and complete final spacing the following spring.

Take care

Do not overwater.

Calendula officinalis 'Fiesta Gitana'

(Pot marigold)

- **Sow in early spring or autumn**
- **Ordinary free-draining soil**
- **Sunny spot**

The newer marigolds, in particular 'Fiesta Gitana', have large double flowers up to 10cm (4in) across. Cream, yellow, gold or orange flowers are formed on compact plants 30cm (12in) high. Stems bear light green leaves, which are long and narrow, and these set off the bright blooms admirably. Apart from their usefulness in the annual border, preferably towards the front, try them in window boxes and other containers. They thrive on poor soil; use them in conditions where other plants may not survive, but make sure such soils are free-draining.

Sow the seeds where they are to flower in early spring, lightly covering them with soil; thin out subsequent seedlings to 15cm (6in) apart. Alternatively sow seed in the usual way during the autumn; such sowings will provide earlier flowers on stronger plants. At the end of each season get rid of any unwanted self-sown seedlings.

Take care

Dead-head to prolong flowering.

Calendula officinalis 'Lemon Gem'

(Pot marigold)

- **Sow in early spring or autumn**
- **Ordinary free-draining soil**
- **Sunny spot**

The very reliable calendulas never cease to delight. The beautiful yellow, orange or gold shades of the flowers are a cheerful sight throughout the season. 'Lemon Gem' has striking double yellow flowers that are formed on compact plants 30cm (12in) high. The long light green leaves are a perfect foil for the bright flowers. Very free-flowering and highly pungent they can be used almost anywhere in the garden.

As this is a hardy annual, seeds can be sown where they are to flower during the autumn or early spring. Take out shallow drills and then lightly cover the seed. Thin out to 15cm (6in) apart. Alternatively, they can be raised under glass to give uniformity for the formal planting areas. Raise during early spring in a frost-free temperature. Autumn-sown plants will be stronger, and flower earlier.

Take care

Dead-head to prolong flowering. 34▶

Callistephus chinensis 'Milady Dark Rose'

(China aster)

- **Sow in early spring**
- **Ordinary well-drained soil**
- **Sunny and open site**

China asters are useful plants for the bed or border, or in containers including window boxes. Recent developments have led to a number of useful additions of the dwarf bedding types, and the cultivar 'Milady Dark Rose' is recommended. The rose-coloured double flowers are borne above the dark green foliage. Plants are about 23cm (9in) high, making them ideal bedding plants especially in areas where wind may cause damage to taller types.

Asters can be affected by various wilt disorders so avoid planting them in the same spot more than once. Sow seed under glass in early spring at a temperature of 16°C (60°F). Use any good growing medium for this purpose, and the subsequent pricking out into boxes. Harden them off in the usual way and plant out into flowering positions in early summer, 15cm (6in) apart.

Take care

Avoid overwatering at any stage. 35▶

Callistephus chinensis 'Milady Mixed'

(China aster)

- **Sow in early spring**
- **Any soil, but well drained**
- **Sunny and open position**

A half-hardy annual, the aster is useful for almost any purpose. Many forms have been developed, from 15cm (6in) high to 75cm (30in). A wide range of colours is available and the shape of the flowers can be just as varied, from button types to large chrysanthemum forms. As a moderate choice try the 'Milady Mixture'. The blooms are slightly incurving and weather resistant, stems are 25cm (10in) high, and the double flowers are in shades of blue, rose, rose-red and white. They are ideal as bedding plants or as drifts in the annual border.

Early flowering plants should be raised under glass in a temperature of 16°C (60°F) during early spring. Sow the seeds in pots or boxes of any good soil-based growing medium. Prick out into boxes, harden off in the usual way and plant out into final positions, 15cm (6in) apart, in late spring or early summer.

Take care

Dead-head to prolong flowering.

Callistephus chinensis Ostrich Plume Mixed

(Annual aster)

- **Sow in early spring**
- **Any well-drained soil**
- **Sunny and open location**

Probably the best of the double strains, the ostrich plume types are earlier flowering than most. The lovely flowers are formed on branching strong stems up to 45cm (18in) high. Each individual bloom is elegantly plumed and can be 10-15cm (4-6in) in diameter. The violet, pink, red, crimson, lavender-blue or white flowers are fairly weather resistant, but remove damaged or dead blooms. Very popular as cut flowers for the house because of their long-lasting qualities, they are also quite at home as bedding plants in a formal bed.

Raise from seed in early spring under glass, in a temperature of 16°C (60°F). Use any good growing medium. Prick off the seedlings in the usual way. Harden off and plant out into flowering positions in early summer at 23cm (9in) intervals.

Take care
Try not to soak the open flowers when watering.

Callistephus chinensis Single Mixed

(Annual aster)

- **Sow in early spring**
- **Any well-drained soil**
- **Sunny and open situation**

Remarkable for their long-lasting qualities in the garden or when cut for floral decoration, these flowers are worth a place in any garden. Petals of the single large daisy-like flowers are carried in two or three rows in shades of pink, red, mauve, blue or purple. The long branching stems can be up to 60cm (24in). Leaves are coarsely toothed, ovate in shape and a good green. Although relatively tall the strong stems should not require support. Keep removing dead flowers so that further buds can develop into new blooms.

Sow seed of this half-hardy annual in spring under glass, in a temperature of 16°C (60°F). Use any good growing medium. Prick out in the usual way and harden off. Plant out into flowering positions in early summer, 23cm (9in) apart.

Take care
To avoid various aster wilts, use a fresh growing site each year.

Campanula medium

(Canterbury bell)

- **Sow in early summer**
- **Rich and fertile soil**
- **Sunny location or partial shade**

This is a biennial of very great merit. If you can afford the space and time to wait it is worthy of a place in any garden.

Flowering in late spring to mid-summer from the previous year's sowing, the upturned bell-shaped flowers are produced in profusion on sturdy plants up to 90cm (3ft) in height. The contrasting foliage is fairly long, wavy edged, hairy and a striking green that sets off the blue, pink, white or violet flowers.

Sow seed in boxes in early summer, prick off the seedlings into individual pots, grow on until the autumn and then plant out into permanent positions; give at least 30cm (12in) space around each plant. Alternatively keep plants growing in pots through the winter and plant out in spring.

This species is very successful in partial shade, but ideally suited to a sunny position.

Take care

Watch for slug damage in winter.

Celosia argentea cristata

(Cockscomb)

- **Sow in early spring**
- **Rich and well-drained soil**
- **Sunny but sheltered position**

As the common name implies the flowers are unusual in being crested in shape. Colours are red, orange, yellow or pink. Stems are up to 30cm (12in) in height and carry light green ovate leaves. These plants can be successfully grown outdoors in the summer. Flowers are at their best from early summer onwards, with crests 7-13cm (2.75-5in) across.

This tender annual requires heat for good germination. Sow under glass in early spring at a temperature of 16-18°C (60-65°F). Use a reliable seed-growing medium. Prick off seedlings into individual small pots for better results. Harden off carefully about two weeks before required for planting. (Should plants look a little starved in the pots, give a weak liquid feed once a week up to hardening off.) Plant out into flowering positions in early summer, or late spring in milder areas. Space at 30cm (12in) intervals.

Take care

Overwatering causes collar rot. 36▸

Celosia argentea pyramidalis 'Apricot Brandy'

(Prince of Wales' feathers)

- **Sow in early spring**
- **Well-drained, fertile soil**
- **Sunny, sheltered location**

Outdoor cultural requirements and propagation are the same as for all celosias. 'Apricot Brandy' was introduced for its dwarf effect: the height at most will be 40cm (16in). A handsome shade of apricot, the plumes are an aggregate of both central and basal side shoots. The plants may have plumes up to 50cm (20in) across, and the light green foliage can be overwhelmed by the bloom.

This cultivar makes an excellent bedding subject for formal plantings, but is also invaluable for displays in window boxes, troughs or containers for the patio or yard. Group together in large pots and place near the front door, to make a pleasant feature for visitors to admire.

Take care

Do not overwater at any stage or plant out too early. 37▸

Celosia argentea pyramidalis 'Pampas Plume Mixture'

(Prince of Wales' feathers)

- **Sow in early spring**
- **Well-drained, fertile soil**
- **Sunny and sheltered spot**

'Pampas Plume Mixture' is worth trying. It has an ideal colour range for the average garden and includes shades of red, yellow, pink and orange. This strain will yield plants up to 75cm (30in), and secondary side shoots will provide a continuing wealth of colour. The feather plumes will themselves measure 10-20cm (4-8in).

As this is a very tender annual, it will require some heat for propagation purposes. Sow seed under glass during early spring in a proprietary peat-based growing medium. Temperatures of 16-18°C (60-65°F) should be maintained. Prick out seedlings into individual pots, and grow on in a warm part of the greenhouse. Harden off about two weeks before planting out into final positions in early summer, 30cm (12in) apart, in a sunny position.

Take care

Do not overwater at any stage.

Centaurea cyanus 'Blue Ball'

(Cornflower; Bluebottle)
- **Sow in autumn or spring**
- **Ordinary well-drained soil**
- **Sunny position**

The common native cornflower is a great favourite, but selection and breeding over many years has led to improved strains for the garden. If you decide to grow this plant, try 'Blue Ball', which is very true to type and free from the purple tinge often found in the blues. Strong 90cm (36in) stems carry the ball-like flowers well above the leaves, which are narrow and lanceolate in shape. Grow in bold groups near godetias and you will have a beautiful contrast of colour during the summer. They are often grown as cut flowers either in the border or in rows in another part of the garden.

Sow seeds in either autumn or spring; those sown in autumn will make larger plants. Take out drills where the plants are to flower, sow the seed and cover. Thin out subsequent seedlings to 45cm (18in). In very cold areas protect autumn-sown seedlings from frost.

Take care
Give support to very tall types. 37▶

Centaurea cyanus 'Red Ball'

(Cornflower)
- **Sow in spring**
- **Ordinary well-drained soil**
- **Sunny site**

This very useful cultivar is an attractive partner to 'Blue Ball' especially if grown for flower arrangements. The individual blooms can be up to 5cm (2in) across, deep red and double. The cultivar has been selected and bred for earliness, and is more suited to springtime sowing, either directly where it is to flower or under glass.

Make first sowings in the greenhouse in early spring in any good growing medium, prick out into boxes and grow on in reduced temperature; harden off and plant out in late spring. Space out to 30-45cm (12-18in).

'Red Ball' is worth a place in the annual border, in combination with plants of similar height.

Take care
Cut off dead flowers to encourage new buds and growth. 37▶

Above: **Borago officinalis**
This tall decorative herb has delightful blue flowers in summer. Young leaves can be used in summer salads and the flowers can be dried for use in potpourris. 25▸

Left: **Brachycome iberidifolia**
Myriads of fragrant daisy flowers cover these compact bushy plants during the summer months. They thrive in the sun but must be sheltered from strong winds. Plant towards the front of the border. 25▸

Right: **Callistephus chinensis 'Milady Dark Rose'**
This dwarf type of China aster bears large, long-lasting blooms. An ideal bedding plant, particularly in windy areas. Good for window boxes. 28▸

Below: **Calendula officinalis 'Lemon Gem'**
Double flowers of a beautiful yellow adorn this compact plant throughout the summer. The calendulas are very reliable annuals and can be used in any sunny area of the garden. 27▸

Left: **Campanula medium**
This old favourite biennial produces large bell-shaped flowers on sturdy plants. Grow in a rich fertile soil for best results and position where it receives some sunshine. This is a single-flowered plant. 30▸

Right: **Centaurea cyanus**
The cultivars 'Blue Ball' and 'Red Ball' are shown here growing together. Excellent for cutting, these are dependable plants for a sunny spot. They thrive in ordinary soil. 32▸

Below: **Celosia argentea pyramidalis 'Apricot Brandy'**
These fine plants revel in a warm and sunny position. Their plume-like flowers last for weeks during the summer, showing up elegantly against the light green foliage. 31▸

Left: **Centaurea moschata 'Dobies Giant'**
Large fragrant flowers in pastel shades adorn this oriental plant in summer. Sow in the border. 49▸

Right: **Chrysanthemum carinatum 'Court Jesters'**
These brightly coloured flowers will last well in water when cut. A very reliable annual for most soils. 50▸

Below: **Cheiranthus cheiri**
Plant these near the house to enjoy their beautiful fragrance on spring evenings. There are many cultivars to choose from, varying in height and colour. Sow the previous summer and protect tall types in winter. 50▸

Above: **Chrysanthemum parthenium 'Golden Ball'**
This compact plant is smothered with bright, button-like blooms for many weeks during the summer. Ideal for borders, tubs and window boxes. 51▸

Below **Cineraria maritima 'Silver Dust'**
The fine silvery foliage provides an excellent foil for summer bedding flowers. Remove the yellow blooms to encourage a neat shape. 52▸

Above: **Cladanthus arabicus**
Orange buds open to golden yellow flowers in endless succession well into the autumn. The plant will thrive in a light soil and a sunny position. The flowers are fragrant. 52◆

Above: **Cobaea scandens**
A vigorous climber for a sheltered sunny spot. The large bell flowers change from green to purple as they mature. Provide support. 54▸

Right: **Cleome spinosa 'Colour Fountain'**
This spectacular plant produces clusters of spidery flowers on tall strong stems. Delicately scented. 53▸

Below: **Clarkia elegans 'Bouquet Mixed'**
These frilly double flowers are long lasting when cut and superb for flower arranging. Grow in sun. 53▸

Above: **Coleus blumei 'Monarch Mixed'**
A large-leaved mixture of rich colour combinations that will thrive in a sheltered sunny position. Pinch out the flowers for compact plants. 55▸

Below: **Convolvulus tricolor 'Rainbow Flash'**
This dwarf hybrid produces bright new flowers each morning; they will fade during the afternoon. Excellent in tubs and window boxes. 56▸

Above: **Collinsia bicolor**
A pretty annual with tiered sprays of dainty bicoloured flowers. It will grow in a damp, partially shaded position. Be sure to provide support for the slender 60cm (24in) stems. 55▸

Above: **Cuphea miniata 'Firefly'**
This bushy, highly branched plant produces clouds of bright scarlet blooms from early summer onwards. Plant in the centre of the border, where it will require no staking. 59▸

Left: **Coreopsis tinctoria 'Dwarf Dazzler'**
A reliable dwarf cultivar with masses of crimson and gold flowers in summer. Will tolerate the polluted atmosphere of towns and cities. 57▸

Right: **Dahlia 'Gypsy Dance'**
A dwarf semi-double strain of bedding dahlia with many new colours on bushy plants. Grow from seed sown under glass in early spring and plant out in early summer. Plants will grow to 60cm (24in). 60▸

Above: **Delphinium consolida 'Tall Double Mixed'**
Tall branching sprays of lovely flowers in many shades for cutting and border display. These are very vigorous plants and need support. 61▸

Centaurea moschata

(Sweet sultan)
- **Sow in mid-spring**
- **Fertile, well-drained soil**
- **Sunny position**

From the Orient, this annual has sweetly scented yellow, purple, pink or white flowers up to 7.5cm (3in) across. Carried on thin stems 45cm (18in) high, the leaves are narrow and their margins tend to be toothed. This species is ideal for the middle of the border, planted in groups.

Plants come into flower in early summer and from this period keep dead blooms picked off, to encourage lower lateral shoots to develop and produce further flowers.

Wherever possible, make sowings directly where plants are to flower, as disturbance can result in considerable losses. To avoid such disappointments sow in drills in mid-spring in a well-drained border, and thin out the germinated seedlings to 23cm (9in) apart. If possible, make a further sowing a month later to ensure a longer period of bloom. The giant strain is well recommended, and has finely fringed petals.

Take care

Avoid replanting seedlings. 38▸

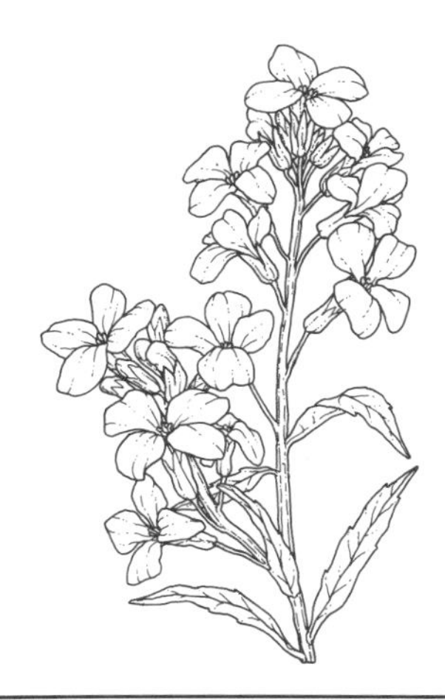

Cheiranthus × allionii 'Orange Queen'

(Siberian wallflower)
- **Sow in late spring or early summer**
- **Almost any soil**
- **Sunny location**

Although it is really a shrubby perennial, the wallflower is short-lived and is better treated as a biennial. The hybrid described here is a beautiful orange. Flowers form in clusters at the end of 38cm (15in) stems on which lanceolate leaves of a good green develop to form a nicely shaped plant.

If your soil tends to be on the acid side, do not despair that the wallflower prefers an alkaline soil; dress the ground with hydrated lime at the rate of 115g per sq metre (4oz per sq yard).

Sow seeds in drills during late spring or early summer. Plant the seedlings in nursery rows 23-30cm (9-12in) apart; put them in their final positions in late autumn. Keep plants watered and hoed throughout the summer.

Take care

Remove damaged stems after winter storms.

Cheiranthus cheiri

(Wallflower)

- **Sow in late spring or early summer**
- **Almost any soil**
- **Sunny position**

This is by far the most popular of spring or early summer bedding plants. Within the wallflower group you can select from many cultivars for both height and colour. All are fairly strongly scented and they give added pleasure if planted near doorways or under windows. The aroma is usually at its best early in the morning or in the late evening. They are quite hardy and come through the worst of winter weather, although heavy snowfall can cause some damage. Ranging in height from 23-60cm (9-24in), the flowers come in a vast range of colours including white, red, yellow and purple. Flowers will appear from mid-spring onwards.

Propagation time and method is the same as that of C. × *allionii*; but when planting out in final positions, give taller types slightly wider spacing.

Take care

In exposed areas give protection to the tall cultivars during winter.

Chrysanthemum carinatum 'Court Jesters'

(C. tricolor)

- **Sow in early spring**
- **Ordinary soil**
- **Sunny position**

This member of the daisy family is one of a number of annual species originating from the Mediterranean area. The plants will grow about 60cm (24in) tall and branch freely under good conditions. The daisy-shaped multicoloured flowers, 5-6cm (2-2.4in) across, open from midsummer onwards and last well when cut. Their varied markings are attractive in an annual border. They will continue to flower until autumn frosts.

Sowings may be direct into flowering position when soil conditions are suitable, in early spring. Thin out seedlings to about 20cm (8in) apart to allow for development. This annual will succeed on most soils given good drainage. The young growths are sometimes attacked by aphids; spray as soon as seen.

Take care

Remove dead flowerheads. 39▸

Chrysanthemum parthenium 'Golden Ball'

(Matricaria eximia)
- **Sow in autumn or spring**
- **Ordinary soil**
- **Sunny position**

'Golden Ball' has similar traits to 'Snow Ball'; it has pungent foliage but is usually grown for the bright colour of its flowers. It is 25cm (10in), slightly shorter than its relative, but it produces a wealth of golden yellow flowers, 2cm (0.8in) across, on firm stems. Avoid very confined or humid conditions, or diseases may occur.

Propagation is the same as for its white counterpart, or alternatively sow seed under glass in spring in a temperature of 13°C (55°F). A good soil-based growing medium will give better results. Prick out in the usual way, harden off in a sheltered frost-free area, and plant out in late spring. This method will ensure an evenly grown batch of plants, essential for formal plantings. Those grown as pot plants should be pricked out singly into individual pots, gradually moving them into larger pots as growth progresses. Spacing in the garden should be 25-30cm (10-12in).

Take care

Spray against pests or disease. 40▸

Chrysanthemum parthenium 'Snow Ball'

(Matricaria eximia)
- **Sow in autumn or spring**
- **Ordinary soil**
- **Sunny position**

This fairly hardy chrysanthemum produces a mass of ivory white flowers with cushion centres, on stems 30cm (12in) tall. Usually flowering from early summer to autumn, the individual blooms are 2cm (0.8in) across. Leaves are very aromatic and light green, making a pleasant foil to the bright flowers. It is suitable for formal bedding, drifts in a border, or containers.

For informal sites sow directly where they are to flower, in spring. Take out shallow drills and just cover the seed lightly. Thin out the seedlings to 30cm (12in). In mild areas sowing can take place in autumn; plants grown in this way will be larger and will flower earlier. Resistance to pests and diseases will also be greater. Because larger plants can be expected, space a little further apart.

Take care

In severe weather protect autumn sowings with polythene tents or cloches.

Cineraria maritima 'Silver Dust'

(Senecio maritimus)
- **Sow in early spring**
- **Ordinary soil**
- **Sunny location**

This plant is grown almost exclusively for its foliage effect in bedding and border arrangements. It is a very fine strain, with intense silver-white foliage deeply dissected, looking like a piece of lace. About 15cm (6in) tall, it makes a pleasing edge to a formal bed.

Only in the mildest areas will this cultivar survive the winter, and therefore propagation is carried out annually. Sow seed during early spring under glass, in a temperature of 16-18°C (60-65°F). Use a good proprietary growing medium for sowing and subsequent pricking out. Grow on in slight heat. Harden off in the usual way before planting out into permanent positions in late spring. Early removal of any flower stems and buds that appear will encourage a finer foliage effect and a better habit of growth.

Take care
Spray against leaf miner. 40▶

Cladanthus arabicus

- **Sow in spring**
- **Light and open soil**
- **Sunny site**

A native of Spain, this lovely annual herb is similar to *Anthemis* but it has the habit of branching just below the flowerheads. It starts to bloom in early summer and will continue well into the autumn; individual flowers are 5cm (2in) across and a deep golden yellow colour. Plants develop into mounds as the season progresses, reaching a height of 75cm (30in). Light green leaves, linear and almost feather-like in shape, make a good foil for the profusion of flowers. Nearly always grown as border plants they are an ideal subject for the centre or rear, adding height and interest to the annual border.

Sow seeds during spring where they are to flower; make sure that ground conditions are fit for this by lightly raking down the soil. Thin out the seedlings when they are large enough to handle, to 30cm (12in) apart.

Take care
Dead-head to prolong flowering. 41▶

Clarkia elegans 'Bouquet Mixed'

(C. unguiculata)

- **Sow in spring**
- **Light to medium soil, slightly acid**
- **Sunny location**

This strain will give a galaxy of double pink, red, white, lavender, purple and light orange flowers. Ovate leaves are carried on branching erect stems of 60cm (24in). The blooms, about 5cm (2in) across, are produced along almost the whole length of the stems, appearing from early summer onwards. Use towards the centre of a border in bold drifts.

Given good weather conditions, sow seed in flowering positions in spring; take out shallow drills, sow thinly and cover. Thin out germinated seedlings to 30cm (12in). Alternatively sow during autumn in mild districts; these will flower the following year from the end of spring onwards. Correct spacing is essential for good growth, and to ensure that disease is kept to a minimum. Grey mould is a particular disease to watch for.

Take care

Avoid over-rich soils, or less flowers will be produced. 42▶

Cleome spinosa 'Colour Fountain'

(Spider plant)

- **Sow in spring**
- **Light, ordinary soil**
- **In full sun**

This is a very exotic, unusual-looking annual; the flowers are spider-shaped and scented. 'Colour Fountain' mixture will include shades of rose, carmine, purple, lilac and pink. Stems reach 60-90cm (24-36in) and carry digitate leaves of five to seven lobes. Some spines may be evident on the undersides of these leaves. This is extremely useful as a 'spot' plant to give height to formal bedding schemes. As a border plant its height will add character, but care should be taken to position it towards the rear in a sunny place.

To flower in summer, seed will need to be sown under glass in spring; use a well-recommended growing medium, and keep at a temperature of 18°C (65°F). Prick out the seedlings into individual pots, 9cm (3.5in) in diameter. Harden off gradually and plant out in late spring. The delicately scented flowers will give great pleasure.

Take care

Check for aphids on young plants. 43▶

Cobaea scandens

(Cathedral bells)
- **Sow in very early spring**
- **Ordinary well-drained soil**
- **Sunny, sheltered location**

Climbers are few among the annuals and biennials, but this glorious flowering climber is quite spectacular. It can be a little temperamental to get into flower, but given good conditions it is worth persevering with. Individual blooms are up to 7.5cm (3in) long, and bell-shaped. Young flowers are a light green, soon changing to violet-purple. The calyx at the base of the bell usually remains green. This vigorous climber can reach a height of 7m (23ft) and is therefore suitable on a wall that has some supports in the way of wires or a trellis.

Grow in a sunny sheltered position for the finest results. Sow seed under glass in early spring, using fresh seed if possible for better germination. Temperature should be maintained at 18°C (65°F). Sow individually in small pots of a good loam-based growing medium. Harden off gradually, and plant out in early summer.

Take care

Water freely in dry weather. 42▸

Coix lacryma-jobi

(Job's tears)
- **Sow in early spring**
- **Any well-drained soil**
- **Sunny, south-facing site**

This is one of a number of annual grasses suitable for beds or borders. The tear-like seeds are grey-green in colour, tiny and pearl-shaped, growing on stems 60-90cm (2-3ft) tall. Similar in habit to sweet corn (*Zea*), they are very vigorous. Once plants are established they will tend to become pendulous before flowering in summer, after which the pearl-like seeds will be formed. If grouped together these plants lend an air of strength to an annual border, and can be accommodated quite happily near very colourful subjects. When ready for harvesting, the hard seeds can be safely used by children for threading onto strings.

Sow seed in early spring under glass, in a temperature of 13-16°C (55-60°F). Use a loam-based compost and sow directly into individual small pots to save later potting on. Plant out into final positions in early summer.

Take care

Avoid overfeeding, or flowering and seed development will be delayed.

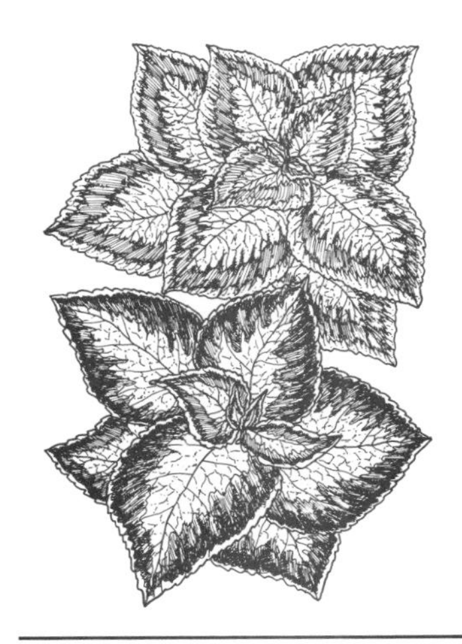

Coleus blumei 'Monarch Mixed'

(Flame nettle plant)
- **Sow in late winter**
- **Ordinary but well-drained soil**
- **Sunny location**

The 'Monarch Mixed' strain is appealing for its wide variation of large coloured foliage; rose, pink, crimson and bronze are the main shades. The bushy plants of nettle-like leaves, up to 45cm (18in) tall, can be put to many uses. Apart from growing as a pot plant they can be safely planted out during the summer months as a bedding plant in formal displays. Drifts in a border can be very effective, too. Window boxes are ideal for this mixture.

Plants are easily grown from seed sown in late winter; use a peat-based growing medium for sowing under glass in a temperature of 16-18°C (60-65°F). Plant single seedlings in individual small pots using a good growing medium. Harden off and set out in final positions in early summer, 30cm (12in) apart. Keep the blue flower spikes pinched out to help the development of compact plants.

Take care

Give container-grown coleus plants a weak liquid feed every 10 days. 44▸

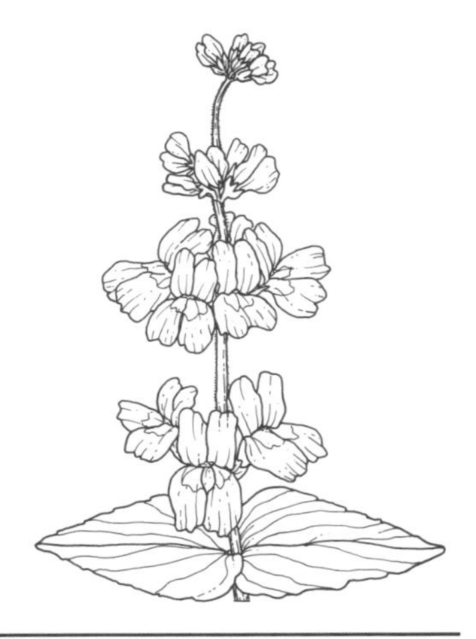

Collinsia bicolor

- **Sow in autumn or spring**
- **Ordinary, moist but well-drained soil**
- **Partial shade**

This very appealing hardy annual can be used in most situations as long as they are not too arid. It is a useful plant because it will tolerate partial shade. It is ideal for the border in a damp shady yard.

Flowers, as its name implies, are two-coloured, having an upper and lower lip formation: the upper petals are usually white and the lower ones lilac to purple. One or two named cultivars are available, mainly pink, and they are worth considering for a change. Their blooms are borne on thin squarish stems carrying lanceolate deep green leaves in pairs. Up to 60cm (24in) in height, they should be grown towards the back of an annual border, preferably near a light yellow subject of a similar height.

Sow seeds where they are to flower, in autumn or spring. Shallow drills will suffice; cover the seeds and thin out when large enough, to 15cm (6in) apart.

Take care

Use bushy peasticks for support. 45▸

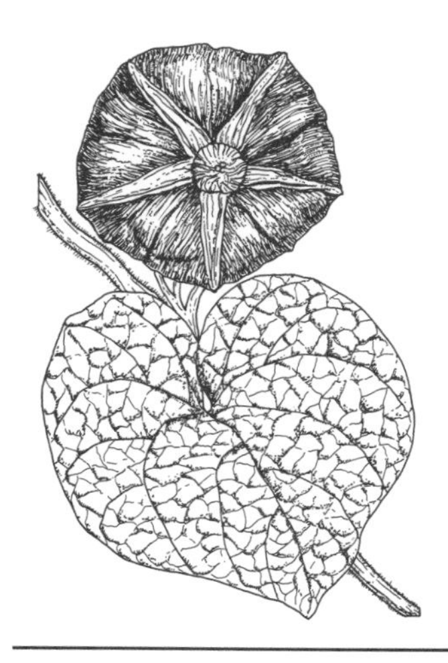

Convolvulus major

(Ipomoea purpurea)

(Morning glory)

- **Sow in spring**
- **Light, rich soil**
- **Sunny but sheltered site**

These annuals will reach a height of 3m (10ft) under normal weather conditions. It is ideal for training on wires or trellis work; use tall peasticks as supports in a border. The lovely flowers, now available in mixed colours, are up to 7.5cm (3in) across and the vine-like stems that twine around the supports are covered with lovely heart-shaped leaves. The trumpet flowers are at their best in the morning and usually close before midday.

Easily grown from seed, this tender annual should be sown in pots of a good growing medium in spring under glass. Maintain a temperature of 18°C (65°F). Use individual pots so that less disturbance is caused at planting time. Place a small cane in each pot when seedlings appear, to support them until setting against permanent supports. Harden off and plant out when the risk of frost has subsided.

Take care

Dead-head to prolong flowering.

Convolvulus tricolor 'Rainbow Flash'

(Morning glory)

- **Sow in spring**
- **Light well-drained soil**
- **Sunny position**

This completely new dwarf hybrid, only 15cm (6in) tall, has a very wide range of colours including blue, purple, pink and rose. The centre of each inflorescence is marked by a star-like form of white or yellow. Because of their dwarf habit, these plants are invaluable for the front of the border or bed, but try them as well in window boxes in a sunny position. If you have a few seedlings left over, pot them into fairly large pots for the patio or conservatory.

Sow seeds under glass in the normal way during spring; it may help germination if you soak the seeds in water for 24 hours before sowing. Keep in a temperature of 18°C (65°F). Harden off and plant out in final positions at the end of spring, 20cm (8in) apart. Water freely during dry weather, especially those plants near the front of a border, where drying out is more likely to occur.

Take care

Keep the temperature constant in the young stages. 44▶

Coreopsis tinctoria 'Dwarf Dazzler'

(Calliopsis)
- **Sow in spring to early summer**
- **Fertile, well-drained soil**
- **Sunny location**

This dwarf cultivar of *Coreopsis* has beautiful daisy-shaped flowers of deep crimson, and each flower is edged with golden yellow, making a vivid contrast. Only 30cm (12in) in height and tending to spread, it is ideally suited to the front of a border or bed in a sunny position. It can also be useful in containers on a patio. An added asset is the remarkable tolerance to smoky environments, and it can therefore be put to good use in industrial towns or cities. Long-lasting and very free-flowering it should be planted in bold groups to get maximum effect.

Wherever you choose to grow these plants, they come readily from seed. Sow in spring to early summer where they are to flower, take out shallow drills and cover seed lightly. If you make later sowings and the weather is dry, then water regularly. Thin out seedlings to 30cm (12in) when large enough to handle.

Take care
Sow only when conditions allow. 46▸

Cosmos bipinnatus 'Candy Stripe'

(Cosmea)
(Mexican aster)
- **Sow in early spring**
- **Light, and also poor soils**
- **Full sun**

The beautiful rose-red and white striped flowers of the cosmos 'Candy Stripe' are very striking, and are a must for any keen gardener. Individual flowers can be almost 7.5cm (3in) across. The intricately cut leaves are formed on branching stems, giving a well-balanced foil to the flowers. Attaining a height of 80cm (32in) and very free flowering, 'Candy Stripe' is most suited to the middle of a border, although it can be used in large pots. It is also excellent as a cut flower.

As it is a half-hardy annual, seed will need to be sown under glass in early spring. Sow in boxes or trays at a temperature of 16°C (60°F). Prick off into small pots, and move on into 13cm (5in) pots of loam-based growing medium when the small pots have filled with roots. Harden off and plant out in late spring, 45cm (18in) apart.

Take care
Stake tall plants before they flower.

Cosmos sulphureus 'Sunny Gold'

(Cosmea)

- **Sow in spring**
- **Light to poor soil**
- **Sunny position**

The varieties of *C. sulphureus* include lemon, yellow and orange-red shades. They are compact, with many single or semi-double flowers on slender stems. The light green pinnate leaves are quite decorative. 'Sunny Gold' is a new dwarf variety with many semi-double golden yellow flowers growing only 30cm (12in) high. The plants are very decorative as a group in a sunny border while the flowers are useful for cutting and displaying indoors.

Sow in seed mixture under glass in 16-18°C (60-65°F). To avoid checks in transplanting, prick seedlings direct into small pots or individual containers. Gradually harden off for planting out in early summer after any danger of frost is past. Space plants about 30cm (12in) apart in groups in a sunny sheltered position.

Take care

Dead-head to prolong flowering.

Crepis rubra

- **Sow in autumn or spring**
- **Ordinary soil, also poor soils if well-drained**
- **Sunny location**

Daisy-shaped flowers appear on leafless stalks around midsummer. The compact plant forms a rosette, the main flowering stem arising from its centre. The mid-green leaves are lanceolate and markedly toothed along the edges. Rose-red or white flowers are produced on the ends of the stems, about 2cm (0.8in) across.

Use this plant in the annual border, between the edge and the centre. The whole plant measures only 30cm (12in) in height. Coming from the mountain regions of the Mediterranean, it is an ideal subject for the rock garden.

Time of sowing will depend on whether you have an area of the garden free from summer plants; if you have, then sowings can be made in autumn. Plants produced from this will be stronger and slightly earlier in flowering. Alternatively, make sowings in spring. In both cases sow where they are to flower and thin out to 15cm (6in) apart.

Take care

Remove dead flowers regularly.

Cuphea miniata 'Firefly'

- **Sow in very early spring**
- **Ordinary soil**
- **Sun or partial shade**

Grown as a half-hardy annual this sub-shrub will do well in most gardens. It spreads to 60cm (24in) and the height is similar. The stems carry green lanceolate leaves, which may be covered with very distinct white hairs. Flowers are formed from the axils of the leaves near the terminals of the stems. Tubular 4cm (1.6in) long scarlet blooms will begin to show colour from early summer and it will flower freely throughout that season.

Treat it as a half-hardy annual for propagation purposes. Sow seed under glass in very early spring, using a soil-based growing medium. Cover the seed lightly in boxes or pots and keep in a temperature of 16°C (60°F). Pot off the seedlings into individual small pots and grow on until early summer, when they should be planted out in flowering positions. Give a weak liquid feed once a week in the seedling stages, starting a month after potting on.

Take care

Plant out when frosts are over. 46◆

Cynoglossum amabile

(Hound's tongue; Chinese forget-me-not)

- **Sow in early or late spring**
- **Rich well-drained soil**
- **Sun or partial shade**

This plant has distinctive turquoise blue flowers like large forget-me-nots. About 45cm (18in) high, the stems form a compact plant. Both stems and leaves will be found to have a downy appearance. The flowers usually appear in midsummer. As a biennial it is most useful in a border, especially if you have an odd corner of dappled shape where other plants have difficulty in getting established. If you have, then make sure plenty of humus is added before seed sowing or planting.

Sow the seeds in drills outdoors in late spring to flower the following year, preferably in nursery beds. Plant out seedlings in nursery rows 15cm (6in) apart. Set out in final positions at the end of autumn. Alternatively, sow under glass in a temperature of 16°C (60°F) during early spring, prick off into boxes or trays, harden off and plant out at the end of spring at 30cm (12in) intervals.

Take care

Do not overwater established plants.

Dahlia 'Dandy'

(Dwarf Collarette)
- **Sow in very early spring**
- **Good moisture-holding soil**
- **Open sunny position**

The various strains of bedding dahlias come into flower quickly from seed. The older forms of collarette dahlias are tall, but 'Dandy' is a dwarf mixture of single flowers in many colours, each having an inner collar of narrow petals. Branched plants reach about 50-60cm (20-24in) with well-formed flowers of 7.5-9cm (3-3.5in) in diameter. The plants do not need support and the elegant flowers are excellent for cutting for indoor display.

Sow seed thinly in seed mixture under glass in very early spring at about 16-18°C (60-65°F). Germination is usually rapid; prick out singly into small pots or peat sections to avoid later disturbance. Grow on in a warm greenhouse until ready for hardening off to plant out in late spring after frosts are past; space about 30-35cm (12-14in) apart. Water freely if necessary until well established.

Take care
Dead-head to prolong flowering.

Dahlia 'Gypsy Dance'

- **Sow in early spring**
- **Free-draining and fertile soil**
- **Sun or partial shade**

Although they are really tuberous perennials, many dahlias are now grown from seed on an annual basis.

The cultivar 'Gypsy Dance' is recommended for growing in beds, borders and containers. Plants attain a height of 50-60cm (20-24in). Leaves range from greens through to deep bronze, forming a striking contrast to the wide range of semi-double blooms, some of which will be 9cm (3.5in) across.

Annual production of dahlias from seed will ensure healthier plants, less prone to the many diseases and virus infections to which named cultivars are susceptible. Quite vigorous in growth this 'bedder' should be sown under glass in early spring at a temperature of 16-18°C (60-65°F) in a peat-based growing medium. Prick out seedlings into individual pots, to ensure an even, vigorous batch of plants. Grow on in a warm greenhouse; harden off about two weeks before planting in final positions at the end of spring or early summer, 30cm (12in) apart.

Take care
Tender; do not plant out too early. 47▸

Delphinium consolida

(Larkspur)

- **Sow in autumn or spring**
- **Rich, well-cultivated soil**
- **Sheltered, sunny position**

Enjoying a position in a sunny sheltered border, larkspur will give great pleasure visually; and the innumerable blooms will enable you to cut for arrangements in the house without having any adverse effect on the garden display. Many individual strains and mixtures are available and all are reliable. Colours include blue, purple, pink, white and red. Single or double flowers are produced on erect stems up to 120cm (48in) tall, in long racemes. The plants spread to about 30cm (12in), and need to be planted towards the back of a border. Leaves are mid-green and deeply cut.

As they are very vigorous in growth, make sure you weed through in the early stages on a regular basis. They can be sown in the open ground in spring, but finer results will be obtained if they are planted in the autumn. Take out drills where plants are to flower, about 30cm (12in) apart, sow seed and cover. Thin out to 30cm (12in) intervals.

Take care

Use peasticks to support tall types. 48◆

Dianthus barbatus

(Sweet William)

- **Sow in early summer**
- **Avoid very acid soil**
- **Sunny location**

The fragrant Sweet William is a useful and cheerful biennial. The plant ranges in height from 30-60cm (12-24in); the flowers are produced in a compact head up to 13cm (5in) across. Single or double blooms open from late spring to early summer and many colours are available, but red and white predominate; bicolours are also common, forming concentric rings in each individual floret.

Stocky plants can be obtained by sowing seeds in a prepared seedbed during early summer. Plant out germinated seedlings into nursery rows 15cm (6in) apart. Keep well weeded throughout the summer. Final positioning, 20-25cm (8-10in) apart, should be carried out during in the autumn. Alternatively, sow where they are to flower, in early summer, and thin out to correct spacing when they are large enough to handle. Avoid very acid soils and dress with lime before the final planting if your soil is of this type.

Take care

In exposed positions use bushy twigs to support the plants. 65◆

Dianthus caryophyllus

(Annual border carnation)

- **Sow in late winter**
- **Most soils, but avoid very acid types**
- **Sunny position**

Up to 45cm (18in) tall, the annual border carnation will add grace to any border as long as the soil is not too acid. They are without doubt an ideal subject for anyone gardening on alkaline soils. Single or double flowers 4-5cm (1.6-2in) across will be produced; stems and leaves are greyish green.

Carnations come readily from seed sown in late winter under glass, in a temperature of 16°C (60°F). Use a good loam-based growing medium, and sow the seed thinly. Prick off the seedlings when they are large enough, and lower the temperature to 10°C (50°F). Plant out towards the end of spring, 30cm (12in) apart. Flowering will commence in early summer. In colder districts it is recommended that sowing takes place in the autumn; winter the young plants through in cold frames and plant out in late spring at similar spacings.

Take care

Do not overwater established plants.

Dianthus chinensis 'Queen of Hearts'

(D. sinensis)

(Indian pink)

- **Sow in spring**
- **Alkaline to neutral soil**
- **Sunny site**

Vibrant scarlet flowers appear in early summer and continue to give pleasure until well into the autumn. Pale green leaves on stems 30cm (12in) long will make for bushy plants.

Adopt one of the following methods for producing plants. Sow seed under glass in spring, using a loam-based growing medium; better results will be obtained if peat is left out of the mixture. A temperature of 13°C (55°F) should be maintained. Prick out seedlings in the usual way and plant out in late spring. Alternatively, sow in mid-spring where the plants are to flower; sow thinly and then space out 15cm (6in) apart. Choose a sunny position for best results. When planting in containers, change the soil each season if you suspect that acid conditions prevail; this will avoid disappointment.

Take care

Remove faded flowers to ensure further growth and blooms.

Dianthus chinensis 'Telstar'

(D. sinensis)

(Indian pink)

- **Sow in mid-spring**
- **Alkaline to neutral soil**
- **Sunny spot**

The brilliant colours of the 'Telstar' F1 hybrids are a must for the keen enthusiast of annual pinks. Only 20cm (8in) in height, the flowers are produced on short stems in late spring or early summer, earlier than most other cultivars. Blooms may be scarlet, crimson, pink, white, picotee or variable stripes. This very free-flowering strain has great appeal, and is well recommended. Use it in borders, in window boxes and other containers, or alongside a path.

Sow where they are to flower, in mid-spring. Take out shallow drills, and only lightly cover the seed. Thin out to 15cm (6in) apart. Alternatively, if you have a greenhouse, then – to be sure of a uniform crop of plants – sow seed in a good loam-based growing medium in a temperature of 13°C (55°F) during spring. Prick out the seedlings into boxes, harden off, and plant out in early summer.

Take care

Make sure your soil is alkaline or neutral for best results. 66▸

Didiscus caeruleus

(Blue lace flower)

- **Sow in spring**
- **Ordinary well-cultivated soil**
- **Sheltered and sunny position**

This lovely half-hardy annual from Australia has the appearance of the perennial scabious. Clusters of delicate lavender-blue flowers are carried on stems 45cm (18in) high. The umbel-shaped inflorescence will appear in midsummer and carry on flowering until autumn. Leaves and stems are covered with masses of tiny hairs, and feel rough to the touch. Choose a sheltered position, preferably towards the front of a border near annuals with white or pale yellow flowers.

Sowing should be carried out during spring under glass, in a temperature of 16°C (60°F). Use a loam-based growing medium for both seed and seedlings. When large enough to handle, the latter will respond better if pricked out into small individual pots. After hardening off, plant them out into final positions, 23cm (9in) apart, towards the end of spring.

Take care

Water well in dry periods. 66▸

Digitalis purpurea

(Foxglove)

- **Sow in early summer**
- **Most soils, but slightly acid**
- **Semi-shade**

This hardy biennial has always been a great favourite. Flowering in the year after sowing, it produces the familiar long spikes, 1-1.5m (3-5ft), bearing tubular flowers of maroon or purple, and distinctly spotted in the throat of each bloom. The common foxglove has for a long time been associated with medicine, but careful selection and breeding has resulted in the introduction of beautiful garden forms of variable colour and size. Outstanding in this respect are the Excelsior hybrid strains. Flower spikes up to 30cm (12in) long arise from a rosette of grey-green leaves at the beginning of summer through to the autumn.

Sow seed in well-prepared seed beds in early summer. Sow seed thinly in drills, and plant out seedlings in nursery rows 15-23cm (6-9in) apart. Plant into final flowering positions in autumn, at 60cm (24in) intervals.

Take care

Water well in dry weather. 67▸

Dimorphotheca aurantiaca 'Dwarf Salmon'

(Star of the Veldt)

- **Sow in early or late spring**
- **Light well-drained soil**
- **Sunny site**

Flowering from midsummer, plants of *D. aurantiaca* need the sunniest. position you can give, otherwise the blooms will not open, especially in shade or dull weather. The cultivar 'Dwarf Salmon' will make a delightful change from the usual range of colours, and its dwarf habit, 23cm (9in), makes it suitable for edging a border or along the side of a pathway, or for an odd gap in the rock garden in full sun. Daisy-like flowers of apricot-pink, about 5cm (2in) across, are formed on short spreading stems carrying obovate leaves, all of which are scented. If possible, plant next to pale blue or white annuals of a similar height, or in front of taller subjects.

Propagation from seed is relatively easy, either under glass during early spring or directly into the open ground in late spring when ground conditions are favourable. Thin out or plant at intervals of 30cm (12in).

Take care

Remove dead flowers regularly. 68▸

Above: **Dianthus barbatus**
These reliable, sweetly scented flowers are great favourites for cutting and summer bedding. Grow as a biennial and support with bushy peasticks. Red predominates. 61▸

Above:
Dianthus chinensis 'Telstar' F1
A very free-flowering dwarf hybrid in many colours that blooms quickly from seed. For the brightest colours grow in sun. Try it in containers. 63▸

Left: **Didiscus caeruleus**
Clusters of delicate lavender-blue flowers are borne on tall stems from midsummer until autumn. Grow in a sunny sheltered spot and be sure to water well during dry spells. 63▸

Right: **Digitalis purpurea**
Tall and stately spikes of spotted flowers adorn these dependable plants. Grown as a biennial, they will thrive in a moist, shady place in the garden. Can be cut for indoors. 64▸

Left: **Dimorphotheca aurantiaca 'Dwarf Salmon'**
A lovely cultivar with apricot-pink 5cm (2in) flowers suitable for edges or the rock garden. It must have full sun for the flowers to open. 64▸

Right: **Eschscholzia californica**
This original Californian annual has been developed into a wide selection of forms and colours. All will give of their best in dry sunny places. Clear self-sown seedlings. 81▸

Below: **Echium plantagineum 'Monarch Dwarf Hybrids'**
A hardy dwarf mixture with flowers of many pleasing pastel shades. Grown in a sunny spot, they will attract hosts of bees during the summer. 81▸

Above: **Exacum affine**
These beautiful little plants with sweetly scented lavender-blue flowers can be planted out in small beds in mild areas. Otherwise, grow in pots in a cool greenhouse. 82▸

Above: **Euphorbia marginata**
Grown for its striking variegated foliage, this plant is well suited to the centre of the border. Superb for flower arrangements when cut. 82▶

Below: **Felicia bergeriana**
A delightful mat-forming plant with masses of miniature, gold-centred, blue, daisy-like flowers in summer. Grow in a sunny sheltered spot. 83▶

Above: **Foeniculum vulgare**
Grow this well-known herb as an annual in mixed borders; its foliage will set off summer flowers. 83▸

Below: **Gazania 'Chansonette'**
A large-flowered hybrid for a sunny position. It will tolerate salty air so is ideal for seaside gardens. 84▸

Above: **Godetia grandiflora 'Dwarf Vivid'**
One of the many lovely single 'Amoena' types available. These hardy annuals are easy to grow and will provide a dazzling display. 84▸

Above: **Godetia grandiflora 'Sybil Sherwood'**
A beautiful single 'Amoena type' with salmon-pink and white blooms. 84▸

Right: **Helichrysum bracteatum**
These papery textured flowers can be cut and dried for decoration. Plant out after the danger of frosts. 86▸

Below left:
Helianthus annuus 'Sungold'
A low-growing sunflower with double blooms 15cm (6in) across. 86▸

Below right: **Helipterum manglesii**
A pink everlasting flower that can be cut and dried for indoors. Sow seed directly into flowering site. 87▸

Left: **Hibiscus trionum**
Each of these beautiful, creamy, dark-centred flowers lasts for one day only but they appear in succession for many weeks from midsummer until late autumn. Grow in sun in any well-drained soil!. 87▸

Right:
Impatiens 'Novette' F1 Mixed
A colourful mixture of glistening flowers for shady or sunny spots in the garden or patio. Plants grow to 10cm (4in) with a wide spread. 89▸

Below: **Iberis umbellata**
Highly fragrant flowers develop quickly on this established favourite. Successive sowings will ensure a long season of colour at the front of the border. Plants will grow and flower well on poor soils. 88▸

Above: **Kochia childsii**
Grown as a half-hardy annual, this is an interesting foliage plant that changes from green during the summer to a rich red as autumn approaches. Use it in borders to add height or as a background. 89▸

Left: **Lagurus ovatus**
An annual grass to add interest to the front of the border. Also suitable for indoor decoration when cut and dried. Do not plant in over-rich soils or in very windy sites. 90▸

Right: **Lathyrus odoratus 'Sheila MacQueen'**
A lovely sweet pea with large waved flowers for exhibition and cutting. Be sure to provide plenty of organic matter in the soil and remove faded flowers regularly. 92▸

Above: **Lavatera trimestris 'Silver Cup'**
A fine hybrid for the garden border or for cutting. Sow in spring or the autumn and space out well. 93▸

Below: **Limnanthes douglasii**
A cheerful hardy annual that will thrive along the edges of a path. The delicately scented flowers will attract bees during the early summer. 93▸

Echium plantagineum 'Monarch Dwarf Hybrids'

(E. violaceum)

(Bugloss)

- **Sow in spring or autumn**
- **Light, dry soil**
- **Open, sunny location**

This member of the borage family produces flowers of an upturned bell shape on the end of light green branching stems. The common species is predominantly blue, but 'Monarch Dwarf Hybrids' have blue, lavender, pink, white and carmine shades, and at only 30cm (12in) tall they require no staking and can be used near the front of a border. The mixture is highly recommended. Choose an open sunny site to ensure free-flowering plants, which will open at the end of spring in mild areas and from early summer onwards elsewhere.

In spring sow seeds where plants are to flower; take out shallow drills and lightly cover the seeds. Thin out to 15cm (6in) apart. Alternatively, sow in autumn in the usual way but wait until spring before thinning out to final distances.

Take care

Do not overwater when plants are established. 68-9▶

Eschscholzia californica

(Californian poppy)

- **Sow in autumn or spring**
- **Most soils, including those considered poor**
- **Sunny and dry position**

In mild areas self-seeding of this annual will produce many plants, but kept under control they are an asset to any garden. Nearly always grown as a border plant, they can be used in the rock garden to good advantage. Choose a sunny position for the best results. Flowers are red, yellow, white, pink and orange. Stems carry deeply cut blue-green leaves. The flower buds have a whorled spike effect and when opened the petals are silky in texture. Double hybrids, listed by many seedsmen, are well worth a try and their frilled blooms are an added attraction. Plants will be 30cm (12in) tall.

Sow in flowering positions in autumn for the best results; the plants that winter through will be stronger and flower earlier. Sow also in spring. In either case thin out the seedlings to 15cm (6in) apart.

Take care

Discard self-sown seedlings at the end of summer. 11, 69▶

Euphorbia marginata

(Snow on the mountain)

- **Sow in mid-spring**
- **Ordinary soil, or poor if well-drained**
- **Sun or partial shade**

The annual species *E. marginata* originates from N America and is grown mainly for its splendid foliage effect; the flowers are very small, white and insignificant. Stems reach a height of 60cm (2ft). The leaves are ovate or oblong, and a pleasant green but with white margins – the terminal leaves may be completely white in some cases. Bracts beneath the flowers are papery in appearance, and also white. On starved soils the foliage colours are intensified. Use this species towards the centre of a border.

Sow seed directly where it is to flower, in mid-spring; thin out the seedlings to 30cm (12in) spacings. Avoid damaging plants, as the milky latex can have an irritating effect on the skin. This euphorbia is ideally suited for flower arrangements; when cutting, place the ends of the stems in very hot water, as this will have a cauterizing effect and seal the flow of latex from the stems.

Take care

Give peastick supports. 71▸

Exacum affine

- **Sow in spring**
- **Ordinary well-drained soil**
- **Sunny and sheltered location**

Only in the mildest areas can this annual be considered for outdoor culture; but if you have such conditions, the exacums are worth considering not just to be different but because of the unusual flowers. They are usually grown as pot plants in the cool greenhouse, but during the summer they can be bedded out in a sheltered border or formal bed. Plants are very compact and bushy, with very shiny deep green ovate leaves. They are only 23-30cm (9-12in) in height. The flowers are 1cm (0.4in) across, saucer-shaped and lavender-blue, with a yellow centre of conspicuous stamens. Once open they are fragrant.

Sow seed in pots or boxes in spring using a good growing medium. Keep at a temperature of 16°C (60°F). Prick out the seedlings into medium pots and grow on until midsummer, when they can be planted out. Spacing will depend on the size of individual plants, but put them as close together as possible.

Take care

Avoid full sun on seedlings. 70▸

Felicia bergeriana

(Kingfisher daisy)

- **Sow in very early spring**
- **Ordinary well-drained soil**
- **Sunny and sheltered position**

The kingfisher part of the common name alludes to the beautiful vivid blue of the flowers. Only 15cm (6in) high, the blooms are carried on short branching stems of a glossy green, as are the narrow grass-like leaves. The single daisy flowers are almost like michaelmas daisies at first glance, about 2cm (0.8in) across, the centre part of the disc being clear yellow. Very compact in habit, they are a choice subject for the front part of a border or rock garden; in either case they need to be sited in full sun.

As this species is a half-hardy annual, propagation will need to be carried out under glass. Sow seed very thinly in pots or boxes of a good loam-based growing medium during very early spring, and keep at a temperature of 16°C (60°F). Prick out the seedlings in the usual way. Reduce the growing temperature at this time and harden off towards the end of spring, when they should be planted out 15cm (6in) apart.

Take care

Pick off dead flowers promptly. 71▸

Foeniculum vulgare

(Fennel)

- **Sow in spring**
- **Ordinary well-drained soil**
- **Sunny position**

As most people know, the herb fennel has a very distinct aroma. The leaves are used – fresh or dried – for flavouring dishes, especially fish and pickles. The seeds, when ripe, are also used for flavouring, and they smell strongly of aniseed. Apart from its culinary uses, fennel can be planted in annual or mixed borders for its foliage. Although perennial in habit, fennel plants can be short-lived, and it is wise to treat them as annuals whatever purpose you use them for. The blue-green leaves, very finely cut and feather-like, are carried on smooth shiny stems 90-240cm (3-8ft) in height. The flowers, which appear in late summer, are a powdery yellow, small and shaped into a flattened umbel about 10cm (4in) in diameter.

Sow the seeds outdoors in spring. Take out shallow drills and lightly cover the seeds with soil. Thin out the seedlings to 23-30cm (9-12in) apart.

Take care

Water well in dry spells. 72▸

Gazania × hybrida 'Chansonette'

(Treasure flowers)

- **Sow in midwinter**
- **Ordinary well-drained soil**
- **Sunny site**

Without doubt this is one of the finest border, bed or rock garden plants, of an almost exotic nature. However only in the mildest parts will they survive winter as a perennial, so they are usually treated as an annual.

Hybrid types carry large daisy flowers, and the 'Chansonette' mixture has a colour range including red, bronze and bicolours. Blooms are carried on short stems 20cm (8in) long and backed by glossy green leaves, but the undersides of white or silver ensure a contrast.

Most useful as a bedder or planted in full sun on the rock garden, they will give an abundance of flower from early summer onwards.

Sow seed under glass in midwinter in a temperature of 16°C (60°F). Use a loam-based compost for sowing, and prick off into individual small pots. Harden off and plant out in early summer, or in late spring in milder districts.

Take care

Make sure ground is free draining to avoid stem and root rots. 72▸

Godetia grandiflora 'Amoena' types

- **Sow in autumn or spring**
- **Light and moist soil**
- **Sunny position**

The 'Amoena' types of godetia are usually taller than the straight 'grandifloras', up to 60cm (24in). Single or double flowers are produced on thin stems, loose in character. Light green lanceolate leaves make an ideal foil for the reddish pink or lilac blooms up to 5cm (2in) across. These are good plants for the centre of a border and they look well in combination with larkspurs. Flowers start to open from early summer onwards. Avoid very rich soils, as these can lead to over-production of foliage to the detriment of the flowerheads. These plants are worthy of a place in any garden, and the profusion of blooms will enable you to cut flowers for arrangements.

Raise from seed in the same way as for the 'Azalea-flowered' types, but space them at 30cm (12in) intervals. Brushwood supports around the plants will help the slender stems to cope with the weight of the flowers.

Take care

Keep moist in dry periods. 73, 74▸

Godetia grandiflora 'Azalea-flowered'

- **Sow in autumn or spring**
- **Light, moist soil**
- **Sunny location**

Of all the hardy annuals godetias are my favourite. The exotically coloured azalea-flowered types are semi-double and have wavy edged petals of pink, salmon, crimson, cerise and white. Almost silky in texture the blooms are produced on branching stems forming a compact plant of about 30cm (12in). The leaves are oblong at the base, narrowing towards the tip; with age they tend to take on a reddish tinge. If these plants are grown next to their near cousins the clarkias, a riot of colour can be expected.

As hardy annuals they are very easy to grow from seed; sow where they are to flower, in either autumn or spring. Plants raised from the autumn sowings will be stronger and will flower slightly earlier, about the end of spring onwards. In either case take out drills, sow seed very thinly, and cover lightly. Thin out the seedlings to 15cm (6in) apart, and water if necessary.

Take care

Keep well watered in dry weather.

Helianthus annuus 'Autumn Beauty'

(Sunflower)

- **Sow in spring**
- **Ordinary soil**
- **Sunny site**

This strain of mixed colours provides an interesting change from the yellow shades of the original types. 'Autumn Beauty' will reach about 180cm (6ft) high and the single flowers include shades of lemon, golden, bronze and mahogany-red; the central brown discs are surrounded by zones of red and brown. Except in exposed positions the plants are sturdy enough to stand without supports.

Seed may be sown direct where the plants are to flower. Sow two or three seeds about 2.5cm (1in) deep, at 30cm (12in) intervals. Thin to one seedling when large enough and protect against slug damage. Choose a position that faces the sun most of the day. Spring sowings should come into flower in late summer and autumn.

Take care

Remove dead heads to encourage further flowering, or leave the nutritious seeds for the birds.

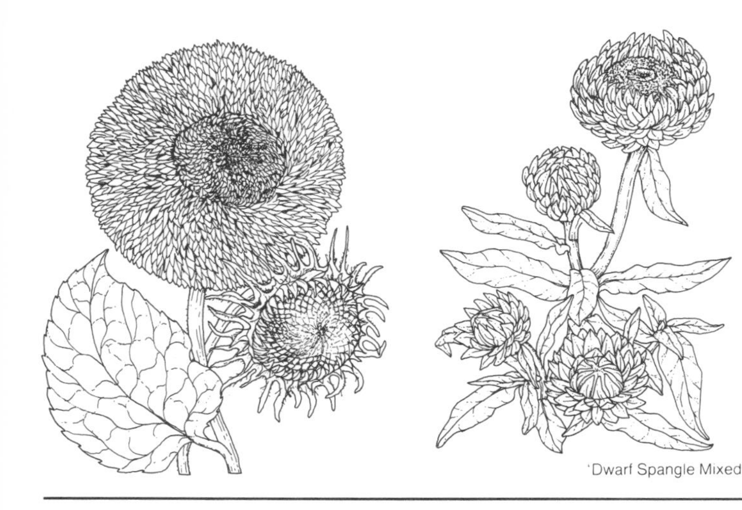

'Dwarf Spangle Mixed

Helianthus annuus 'Sungold'

(Sunflower)

- **Sow in spring**
- **Ordinary soil**
- **Sunny position**

So many people grow the giant exhibition types of this annual that it is often forgotten that a number of the same sunflowers have dwarf counterparts that are easier to cope with.

'Sungold', only 60cm (24in) tall, can have a worthy place in any border as long as it can benefit from a sunny position. The beautiful double golden-yellow blooms can be up to 15cm (6in) across, and almost ball-shaped. The short stems and longish leaves feel coarse to the touch; the latter have toothed margins. More showy when grown in groups, they are best suited to the front of a bed.

Sow seed directly into the ground where they are to flower, putting three seeds to a station; when germination is complete, discard the two weakest seedlings, leaving only the strongest. Spacing should be 30cm (12in). In mild areas sow in spring; for other districts, late spring.

Take care

Check carefully for slug damage at germination time. 74▸

Helichrysum bracteatum

(Everlasting flower)

- **Sow in very early spring**
- **Light but well-drained soil**
- **Sunny location**

These come in a wide range of colours, and there are both tall and dwarf strains available. Stems may be up to 90cm (36in), fairly stiff and branching, and of a light green colour, as are the lanceolate leaves. Flowers are produced terminally on the stems in shades of red, yellow, pink, orange and white, up to 5cm (2in) across. The centre of each bloom is surrounded by a mass of coloured bracts of a papery texture.

Cut stems for drying before the flower centres are fully open and hang them upside down in a cool airy place away from strong sunlight, which may bleach the colours.

Sow seed under glass in very early spring at a temperature of 18°C (65°F); use a loam-based growing medium for sowing and subsequent pricking off. Harden off carefully and plant out at the end of spring. Blooms appear from early summer onwards.

Take care

Use brushwood supports around the groups of plants. 75▸

Helipterum manglesii

(Rhodanthe manglesii)

- **Sow in spring**
- **Poor or ordinary but free-draining soil**
- **Sunny position**

This is another everlasting flower of merit. Growing 30-60cm (12-24in) high, it is an ideal subject for a single small bed; use a few spot plants through the bed to give extra height. Flowers are mainly pink, white and shades of red, about 2.5cm (1in) in diameter. The dainty bracts supporting the blooms terminate on single glaucous stems. Cut the stems for future use before the bracts are fully open; in this way they will keep their colour longer. Avoid strong sunlight in storage.

Sow directly where they are to flower, during spring, lightly covering the seed. Thin out to 15cm (6in) apart. Alternatively raise under glass in the usual way during early spring at a temperature of 16°C (60°F). Plant out carefully at the end of spring. Losses may occur when transplanting, as helipterums do not take kindly to disturbance, so whenever possible sow directly into flowering position.

Take care

Free-draining soil is essential. 75▸

Hibiscus trionum

(Bladder ketmia)

- **Sow in spring**
- **Ordinary well-drained soil**
- **Sunny location**

This exquisite half-hardy annual from Africa blooms continuously from midsummer through to the end of autumn. The delicate exotic flowers are up to 7.5cm (3in) across, white to pale yellow with a chocolate-maroon centre. Stems bearing these beautiful flowers, up to 75cm (30in) long, are a lovely dark green, with ovate leaves that are toothed along the margins. Individual flowers usually last for only one day, but they are eventually followed by an inflated bladder-shaped calyx that will cause interest.

To obtain early-flowering plants, sow seed in pots or boxes in spring; use any good growing medium. When seeds have germinated, prick off seedlings into individual small pots, harden off in a cold frame and plant out at the end of spring. Plants produced in this way will flower earlier than those directly sown in mid-spring. For both methods space the young plants 30cm (12in) apart.

Take care

Check young plants for aphids. 76▸

Iberis amara

(Giant candytuft)

- **Sow from spring onwards**
- **Ordinary or poor soil**
- **Sunny position**

This is one of a number of candytufts of an annual character, grown for its fragrance and ease of cultivation. At about 38cm (15in) tall, blooms are formed in clusters of pure white flowers 5cm (2in) in diameter.

This is an ideal subject for towns and cities where the atmosphere is smoky, as they tolerate such conditions very well. Try them in window boxes if you have no border; containers are ideal for growing this common but lovely plant. Along the edge of pathways the appealing fragrance will be an added bonus as long as the plant is in full sun.

Raise plants in the same way as for *I. umbellata* and thin out in the border to the same spacing. These easy plants are generally free of disease and will thrive on poor soils.

Take care

Remove dead flowers as soon as possible to extend blooming.

Iberis umbellata

(Candytuft)

- **Sow from spring onwards**
- **Ordinary or poor soil**
- **Sunny situation**

Many gardeners will recall candytuft as among the first plants that they grew in a small plot as children. Still very popular, this strongly aromatic hardy annual looks good along the edge of a well-used pathway where its scent can be appreciated. Use it also in bold drifts towards the front of a border.

Umbel-shaped flowers form in clusters up to 5cm (2in) across, on stems 15-38cm (6-15in) high, from early summer to the autumn. The colours are purple, rose-red and white. Leaves are green, lanceolate and slender-pointed, and may be smothered by the profusion of blooms. As flowering is quick from seed, successive sowings will help to prolong the season of flowering.

Sow thinly where they are to flower, in spring. Seedlings should be thinned to 15cm (6in) spacing. It is essential to carry out this process correctly if overcrowding and losses are to be avoided.

Take care

Keep removing dead flowers. 76◆

Impatiens 'Novette' F1 Mixed

(Busy Lizzie)

- **Sow in mid-spring**
- **Ordinary but fertile soil**
- **Shade, semi-shade or sunshine**

During the last decade, busy Lizzies have been developed to suit almost any position and conditions. They are very versatile, and can be safely used in difficult shady parts of the garden or in full sunshine: not many half-hardy annuals tolerate both.

So many cultivars or hybrids are available that it is difficult to make a choice, but the very dwarf 'Novette' mixture, with plants only 10cm (4in) high, is well worth considering.

As a tender half-hardy annual, it will need to be raised under glass. Sow seed on a peat-based growing medium and lightly cover, in spring. Keep at a temperature of 18°C (65°F); if it falls below this, then germination will be difficult and uneven. When they are large enough to handle, prick out the seedlings into boxes of a peat-based growing medium. Harden off gradually and plant out in final positions in early summer.

Take care

Do not plant out too early. 77▸

Kochia trichophylla childsii

(Burning bush)

- **Sow in spring**
- **Fairly light, open soil**
- **Sunny location**

Fine foliage is always welcomed in the garden and kochias are excellent for providing it. Half hardy in habit, these plants will reach 1m (39in) in height in the one season. Each plant consists of a multitude of fine narrow pointed light green leaves; the flowers are also green, but small and inconspicuous. The whole plant will change its colour to a beautiful deep rich red towards autumn, and hence the common name of this most useful species. Although it is relatively tall, the compactness of its habit makes staking unnecessary.

Propagation is fairly easy and should be carried out in spring. Sow seeds in pots or boxes of a good growing medium, in a temperature of 16°C (60°F). Pot seedlings into individual medium-size pots and grow on at a reduced temperature. Harden off in the usual way and plant out into final positions at the end of spring at 60cm (24in) intervals.

Take care

Remember proportions when planting with other subjects. 78▸

Lagurus ovatus

(Hare's tail grass)

- **Sow in late summer or early autumn**
- **Ordinary well-drained soil**
- **Sunny position**

This beautiful annual grass is of medium height, 30cm (12in), with a very attractive inflorescence. The almost white ovate flowerheads appear from early summer through until autumn. As the common name implies its shape is somewhat like that of a hare's woolly tail. The greenish grey foliage is linear, and gives a good contrast to the fine flowers. Grow near the front of a bed or border where the plants will be admired at their best. As with all grasses, avoid over-rich soils, which can lead to fungal diseases.

Although seed can be sown directly into flowering positions, better results will be obtained if seed is sown into boxes during late summer or early autumn in a cool greenhouse. Prick out the seedlings into clumps in boxes of loam-based growing medium. Grow on through the winter and keep protected only from the severest weather. Plant out in mid-spring 15cm (6in) apart.

Take care

Avoid very windy positions. 78▸

Lathyrus odoratus 'Jet Set Mixed'

(Sweet pea)

- **Sow in autumn or spring**
- **Ordinary but fertile soil**
- **Sunny sheltered position**

The intermediate types of sweet pea have been bred to provide many of the improved characters of the taller types but with a more compact habit of growth.

The flowers of 'Jet Set Mixed' include a range of bright colours, with 5 or 6 blooms on stems long enough for cutting. The plants are freely branching, but reach only 90cm (3ft) high. Canes may be placed around them for neatness, if desired; otherwise they need no support.

Sow seeds in autumn or spring direct where they are to flower, if conditions are suitable. Alternatively sowing under cold glass would provide some earlier flowers. 'Jet Set' would make an interesting group in a small separate bed or as a feature in a large mixed border. The plants usually break freely without pinching.

Take care

Watch out for aphids and spray with a suitable insecticide.

Lathyrus odoratus 'Leamington'

(Sweet pea)
- **Sow in autumn or spring**
- **Ordinary but fertile soil**
- **Sunny sheltered spot**

Very sweetly scented, the cultivar 'Leamington' has exquisite lavender fairly weatherproof flowers. If you are growing them for exhibition, they should be treated as single cordons; single stems will need to be trained on individual canes or wires. Side shoots formed in the axils of the leaves, together with tendrils, will need to be removed at an early stage so that as much energy as possible is used in the production of high-quality blooms.

Plants are raised from seed (peas) sown in autumn or spring in pots or boxes of a loam-based growing medium. If autumn-sown, they will require no heat for germination. In spring under glass keep in a frost-free temperature until hardening off has been completed. Better results are obtained from the overwintered plants from autumn sowings. Plant out in spring at 15-23cm (6-9in) intervals.

Take care
Remove faded flowers promptly.

Lathyrus odoratus 'Red Arrow'

(Sweet pea)
- **Sow in autumn or spring**
- **Ordinary but fertile soil**
- **Sunny sheltered site**

'Red Arrow' is a recent introduction and has great potential. Very large scarlet flowers are produced on good solid stems. As the petals are quite firm in texture they are reasonably weatherproof. This vigorous cultivar will need space.

For ordinary garden purposes sow seeds in early spring in the area where they are to flower. Sow them 10cm (4in) apart and 2.5cm (1in) deep. Thin out or transplant seedlings to 23cm (9in) apart. Alternatively sow in the autumn into boxes; prick out seedlings into individual small pots. When three pairs of leaves have been developed, pinch out the growing point; this will encourage growth to become bushy later on. Grow on through the winter in a cold frame and protect from the severest weather only. Plant out in early spring. Use peasticks, wires, trellis or canes for support.

Take care
Soak seeds in cold water overnight before sowing, to assist germination.

Lathyrus odoratus 'Sheila McQueen'

(Sweet pea)

- **Sow in autumn or spring**
- **Well-drained, medium loam**
- **Sunny but sheltered location**

'Sheila McQueen' is a lovely shade of salmony orange with a pink tint showing through; a creamy base is also apparent. For ordinary garden purposes let them ramble over trellis work or arches, or provide a wigwam of peasticks in the annual or mixed border.

Dig in plenty of organic matter before planting, to provide for a cool root run by retaining moisture at the hottest times of the year. Sow the seed (peas) in autumn or spring; those sown in autumn will flower earlier. To help the seed to germinate, nick the hard outer casing of the seed or soak it in water for 24 hours before sowing in a loam-based growing medium. Use pots or boxes for sowing and then place the seedlings singly in small pots. Autumn sowings need to be placed in a cold frame; those sown in spring must be kept in a temperature of 16°C (60°F). Plant out in early spring, 15cm (6in) apart.

Take care

Remove faded flowers regularly. 79▸

Lavatera trimestris 'Alba'

(White mallow)

- **Sow in autumn or spring**
- **Ordinary soil**
- **Sunny and sheltered location**

The white mallow has attractive trumpet-shaped flowers up to 10cm (4in) in diameter. The intensely white satiny petals that make up each individual bloom will give lasting pleasure. Self-supporting stems up to 1m (39in) will be covered in a profusion of flowers if given the right growing conditions. Blooms are produced from the axils of the deep green lobed leaves from early summer onwards. Plant breeders have developed a number of strains. Whichever you choose remember that they are vigorous and will need plenty of space to establish themselves. They are ideal for planting in a border, especially against a wall of a contrasting colour.

Produce plants in the same way as for *L. trimestris* 'Silver Cup'. Mallows self-seed very readily and it is wise to weed out those not required at the end of each season; otherwise, unwanted plants could choke other subjects.

Take care

Plant in a sheltered position.

Lavatera trimestris 'Silver Cup' (L. rosea)

(Mallow)

- **Sow in autumn or spring**
- **Ordinary soil**
- **Sunny and sheltered spot**

Mallows have long been grown for their attractive free-flowering effects. The annual cultivar 'Silver Cup' recommended here is one of a number of new hybrids recently developed from *L. rosea.* Glowing pink blooms 7.5-10cm (3-4in) in diameter are freely produced on stems 60-70cm (24-28in) high and spreading to 75cm (30in). This plant is a member of the hollyhock family, and its leaves are a good green, ovate and lobed. Flowers grow from the leaf axils and are trumpet-shaped, almost satin in texture, and very pleasing to the eye. Apart from their use in the perennial border, try them towards the back of an annual border.

Sow seed directly where plants are to flower, in autumn or spring, and cover lightly. Thin out the seedlings of either sowing during late spring to 45cm (18in) intervals. The strong low branching habit of this plant requires no staking.

Take care

Give plants plenty of space. 80▸

Limnanthes douglasii

(Poached egg flower)

- **Sow in spring**
- **Ordinary soil**
- **Sunny position**

This is popularly known as poached egg flower because of its blooms, which have yellow centres surrounded by white. Each flower is saucer-shaped, and the blooms are produced on 15cm (6in) stems with deeply cut light green leaves. The blooms open in early summer, and are 2.5cm (1in) across. Bees have a particular liking for the flowers of this plant, which are delicately scented, and they can nearly swamp the plants. Apart from their outdoor use these plants can give a succession of colour in a cool greenhouse or conservatory during winter or spring; seed for this should be sown in early autumn.

For flowering in the garden, sow seeds where they are to flower, in spring. In milder areas autumn sowings will produce earlier flowering plants. Only just cover the seed with fine soil, and later thin out seedlings in both methods to 10cm (4in) intervals.

Take care

Discard self-sown seedlings. 80▸

Limonium sinuatum 'Gold Coast'

(Statice sinuata)

(Everlasting flower)

- **Sow in very early spring**
- **Ordinary soil**
- **Open, sunny position**

Formerly known as *Statice*, this everlasting flower has long been popular for its papery blooms in white, yellow, rose and blue. The cultivar 'Gold Coast' has excellent bright yellow flowers, which are produced on slightly winged green stems 60cm (24in) high, of erect habit. Formed in clusters up to 10cm (4in) long, the blooms appear in midsummer.

Sow seed under glass in very early spring at a temperature of 16°C (60°F). The seeds will be slightly clustered and will need teasing apart so that individual seeds can be sown; if this task is carried out, patience will be well rewarded by more even germination, and growth will be more rapid. Use a good loam-based growing medium for seeds and pricking out. Harden off in the usual way and plant out at 30cm (12in) intervals in early summer.

Take care

Do not disturb when planted. 97▸

Linaria maroccana

(Toadflax)

- **Sow in mid-spring**
- **Ordinary, preferably gritty soil**
- **Sunny location**

These dainty antirrhinum-like flowers with a short spur will provide a wealth of colour in almost any part of the garden as long as the site is sunny and well-drained. Flowers are produced on shortish stems in the form of a spike; 30cm (12in) is about the average height. They come in a variety of colours; the lower lip of each bloom is usually marked with a white or pale yellow blotch, resulting in a complete contrast to the upper petals. About 1cm (0.4in) long, the flowers are supported by pale green leaves of a linear shape.

Seedlings can be temperamental when moved and it is advisable to sow seeds where they are to flower. Sow in very shallow drills in mid-spring, covering the seeds lightly. If growing on a dry wall then mix the seeds with a little peat and push into the crevices; hold them in place with a little damp moss. Thin out seedlings elsewhere to 15cm (6in).

Take care

Do not overwater mature plants. 98▸

Linaria reticulata 'Crimson and Gold'

(Portuguese toadflax)
- **Sow in mid-spring**
- **Ordinary soil**
- **Sunny position**

This crimson and gold cultivar has been developed from the very tall Portuguese toadflax; its reduced height, 30cm (12in), makes it easier to deal with in the garden. Gold-splashed scarlet-crimson flowers, resembling snapdragons with a short spur, open from late spring and are 2cm (0.8in) long. The compact plants, made up of pale green, linear leaves holding spiky flowerheads, can be put to good use in the annual border. Try also to sow directly into containers on a patio in full sunshine. At the end of each season discard any self-sown seedlings.

As a hardy annual and for ordinary garden purposes, sow the seeds in spring in shallow drills where they are to flower, and only lightly cover the seed. Thin out the seedlings to 15cm (6in) apart. Further sowings at monthly intervals to the end of spring will ensure a succession of flowering over a longer period.

Take care

Keep well weeded when young. 99▸

Linum grandiflorum 'Rubrum'

(Scarlet flax)
- **Sow in autumn or spring**
- **Ordinary well-drained soil**
- **Full sun**

Waving in a light summer breeze this hardy annual is splendid if you can give it the correct cultural conditions. The scarlet saucer-shaped flowers are up to 5cm (2in) across, on wispy 30cm (12in) stems of a light green; the narrow leaves are in sympathy with the light airy feeling of this plant. The slightest air movement will set the flowers in motion. Use in conjunction with a pale contrasting-coloured annual, towards the front of a border.

Sow directly where they are to flower – during spring in most areas, but milder districts can take advantage by sowing in the autumn, which will produce flowers earlier on stronger plants. Broadcast the seed over the chosen area and rake in lightly. Thin out seedlings to 15cm (6in) apart.

Other, usually taller, cultivars of *L. grandiflorum* are available.

Take care

Seeds can rot before germination if the site is not well drained. 98-9▸

Lobelia erinus 'Colour Cascade Mixed'

- **Sow in late winter or early spring**
- **Ordinary well-cultivated soil**
- **Sun or partial shade**

Probably one of the most widely grown half-hardy plants, lobelia has many uses. It includes many shades of blue, rose, red, mauve and white eyed flowers, which continue to appear until cut down by autumn frosts.

Although best results are obtained from planting in sunny positions, lobelias also succeed in partial shade. These tender perennials need to be sown in heat in late winter or early spring to obtain maximum results. Sow the small seeds very thinly on the surface of a moistened peat-based seed mixture and do not cover. Germinate in a temperature of 18-21°C (65-70°F). Water carefully to avoid disturbance. Prick out as soon as the seedlings can be handled, either singly or in small clumps. Grow on in cooler conditions when established and harden off to plant out when risk of frost has passed.

Take care

Keep the plants watered in dry weather, and fed at intervals. 100▸

Lunaria annua

(L. biennis)

(Honesty; Moonwort)

- **Sow in late spring or early summer**
- **Light soil**
- **Partial shade**

This hardy biennial from the cabbage family starts to flower quite early, usually from mid-spring onwards. Individual blooms are made up of four petals in a cross shape, in shades of purple and white; some crimson can appear in mixtures. The flowers are followed by flattened disc-like seedpods highly prized for floral art work. Blooms and seedpods are formed on stems up to 75cm (30in) long, carrying heart-shaped leaves of a dark green. Grow towards the back of a border, but also make use of its tolerance to partial shade.

Sow seeds in nursery rows during late spring. Thin out the seedlings to 15cm (6in) apart, still in nursery rows. Plant out into final positions in the autumn at 30cm (12in) intervals.

If storing the seedpods, cut the stems in late summer when the pods are still slightly green. The clear silver discs are easily damaged by strong winds.

Take care

Keep slugs at bay. 100▸

Above: **Limonium sinuatum 'Gold Coast'**
This yellow-flowered cultivar has papery blooms that will dry well if cut before they are fully open. Many other colours are available. 94◆

Left: **Linaria macroccana 'Fairy Bouquet'**
This dwarf variety grows to about 20cm (8in) in height and produces a most attractive mixture of colours. Grow in sun and in a very well-draining soil for best results. 94▸

Right: **Linaria reticulata 'Crimson and Gold'**
At 30cm (12in) high this is a useful and pretty plant for the annual border. It will also thrive in containers on a sunny patio. 95▸

Below: **Linum grandiflorum 'Rubrum'**
This hardy annual should be sown directly into its flowering position. The bright scarlet flowers are produced throughout the summer. Combine with paler plants. 95▸

Left: **Lunaria annua**
These hardy, early flowering plants grow well in partial shade and poor soils. The cross-shaped blooms give way to flattened seedpods much in demand for indoor decoration; cut in late summer before they ripen. 96▸

Right: **Lupinus hartwegii 'Pixie Delight'**
A dwarf form of annual lupin with pretty mixed flowers that will provide colour well into autumn. These plants will not need support. 113▸

Below:
Lobelia erinus 'Colour Cascade'
A pleasing blend of trailing varieties for hanging baskets, window boxes and low walls. Grow in full sun and give a weak liquid feed every ten days to sustain flowering. 96▸

Above: **Matthiola incana 'Giant Imperial Mixed'**
This is a fine mixture of these sweetly scented garden favourites. The flowering stems will grow to a height of about 50cm (20in). 114▸

Left: **Malope trifida 'Grandiflora'**
This vigorous branching annual will make a bold splash of colour in a large border. It will thrive in a light soil and a sunny location. Also suitable for patio containers. 113▸

Right: **Mentzelia lindleyi**
These lovely golden yellow flowers revel in the sun; they are scented and appear in profusion throughout the summer months. Be sure to water well in dry periods. 115▸

Above left:
Mesembryanthemum criniflorum
These free-flowing plants are ideal for carpeting a dry sunny site. 115▸

Above: **Mimulus variegatus**
In moist situations these compact plants will produce their masked and spotted flowers until autumn. 117▸

Left:
Mesembryanthemum 'Lunette'
A new, early flowering cultivar of this lovely established plant. 116▸

Below:
Myosotis alpestris 'Ultramarine'
The deep blue flowers will blend with spring-flowering bulbs. 117▸

Above: **Nemesia strumosa 'Fiesta'**
A lovely mixture of unusual colours for small beds and containers. Grow nemesias in a sunny place and keep moist in hot dry weather. Make a second sowing for a long display. 118▶

Left: **Nemophila menziesii**
The spreading habit of this hardy annual makes it ideal for planting along the edge of a border. It will tolerate partial shade as well as sun. About 23cm (9in) high. 118▶

Right: **Nicandra physaloides**
This tall, branching annual should be given adequate space to develop. The flowers are produced over many weeks but open only for a few hours during the middle of the day. 119▶

Above: **Nicotiana 'Crimson Rock' F1**
This free-flowing compact variety has beautifully fragrant blooms. 119▸

Right: **Nigella damascena 'Persian Jewels'**
Delicate semi-double blooms in shades of blue, pink and white. 121▸

Below:
Nicotiana 'Nicki F1 Hybrids'
A colourful mixture of fragrant blooms borne on dwarf plants. 120▸

Above: **Papaver somniferum 'Paeony-flowered Mixed'**
These very decorative poppies from the Orient and the Mediterranean provide a short-lived but extremely colourful show in early summer. 122▸

Right: **Perilla nankinensis**
This half-hardy annual provides a rich backdrop of dark foliage. 123▸

Below: **Petunia 'Resisto Rose' F1**
A lovely free-flowering hybrid. 124▸

Above: **Phacelia campanularia 'Blue Bonnet'**
An easily grown, true blue hardy annual for early flowering. The fragrant blooms will attract bees. Ideal for edging a garden path. 124▶

Lupinus hartwegii 'Pixie Delight'

(Lupin)

- **Sow in autumn or spring**
- **Neutral or acid and poor soil**
- **Sun or partial shade**

Handsome spikes of this popular annual will give long-lasting colour in the average garden throughout the summer. 'Pixie Delight' will give shades of pink, purple, blue and red, on stems 45cm (18in) high, from early summer to late autumn. The plants of this mixture do not need staking. Frequently used to fill gaps in mixed or herbaceous borders, they look just as well in a bed or border on their own. Plant them also in containers for the patio or yard. An abundance of seedpods can be produced and it is wise to remove these if you have young children, as tummy upsets may occur if they eat the small peas or pods. To be safe, cut off the flowerhead as soon as the colour has faded.

Plants are easily raised from seeds, sown directly where they are to flower in autumn or spring. Autumn-sown plants will be earlier to flower and somewhat larger. Thin out seedlings to 23cm (9in) apart.

Take care

Fork peat into alkaline soil. 101◆

Malope trifida 'Grandiflora'

(Mallow wort)

- **Sow in mid-spring**
- **Light soil**
- **Sunny position**

This annual of a very distinctive nature comes from Spain. Its richly coloured flowers will enhance any sunny border. Once established the plants, up to 1m (39in) tall, will provide wide trumpet flowers of a light purple with internal veins of a deep almost black-purple, up to 7.5cm (3in) across, borne on erect branching stems with lobed green leaves. They make compact plants, and will require no staking despite their height. In large borders use them near a pale yellow or white annual. Container-grown for the patio they will give height to a somewhat flat area.

As this is a hardy annual it is not necessary to propagate it under glass, but simply sow the seeds where they are to flower. Carry out the usual process in mid-spring and thin out seedlings to 15-23cm (6-9in) apart. The flowers will appear from early summer onwards.

Take care

Discard unwanted self-sown seedlings. 102◆

Matthiola incana Dwarf Ten Week Stock

- **Sow in spring**
- **Most soils, preferably alkaline**
- **Sun or partial shade**

These flowers, on 25cm (10in) stems, and in a splendid range of red, pink, rose, carmine and purple, will be long lasting. Blooms appear about 10 days before other cultivars of the type.

Correct cultural conditions are essential to obtain maximum results. Sow under glass in early spring at a temperature of 18-21°C (65-70°F). Use a sterile growing medium to avoid damping-off disease. When germination has been completed reduce the temperature to 10°C (50°F). If you grow the selectable strains, you can discard the dark types and prick off the light ones; this will ensure that most will be double flowered. When handling young seedlings, hold by the edge of a leaf and not by the sensitive stem, which could be damaged and rot. Plant out after hardening off, at 23cm (9in) intervals.

Take care

Lime the soil before planting, if it is too acid.

Matthiola incana 'Giant Imperial Mixed'

- **Sow in early spring**
- **Most soils, preferably alkaline**
- **Sunny position, but tolerates partial shade**

Stocks must be one of the most popular scented annuals. *En masse* this fragrance can be overpowering, however, so do not overplant. The 'Giant Imperial mixture' always provides reliable flowers with a high percentage of doubles. Stems 38-50cm (15-20in) tall carry a profusion of pink, white, lilac, purple and crimson spikes of flowers from early summer onwards. Grey-green soft narrow leaves are formed under the flowerheads and give a pleasing contrast.

Sow seed for summer flowering during the early spring under glass in a temperature of 13°C (55°F). Use a loam-based mixture for sowing and pricking off seedlings. Grow on in a lower temperature, and harden off before planting out 23cm (9in) apart.

Take care

Kill caterpillars at once. 102-3▸

Mentzelia lindleyi

(Bartonia aurea)

(Blazing star)

- **Sow in early spring**
- **Light and fertile soil**
- **Sunny position**

Known in the past as *Bartonia aurea*, this beautiful annual has lovely golden-yellow flowers resembling the common St John's wort; the masses of stamens in the centre of each bloom are surrounded by five large petals. Fleshy stems carry a profusion of flowers from early summer, up to 45cm (18in) high; the leaves are a lovely foil, and are somewhat narrow and deep green. The choice of site is important as mentzelias love the sun; plant them between the front and the centre of an annual or mixed border. Sweetly scented, they can be used in patio borders, or try them in window boxes, but remember that they may block out some of your indoor light.

As they are hardy annuals sow them directly where they are to flower, in early spring. Take out shallow drills and sow the seed, cover over lightly and water if necessary. The resultant seedlings should be thinned to 23cm (9in).

Take care

Water well in dry periods. 103▸

Mesembryanthemum criniflorum

(Livingstone daisy)

- **Sow in spring**
- **Most soils, including poor ones**
- **Full sun**

This plant originates from S Africa, and a sunny warm position is essential for good flowering. Prostrate in growth but tending to trail, it is an ideal subject for the front of a window box, over a low dry stone wall, or as a drift near the front of a border. Stems are fleshy, green to reddish in colour, with cylindrical leaves. Flowers are up to 4cm (1.5in) across and appear in a multitude of colours including white, orange, red, pink; a number will be bicolours with a white centre.

This tender fleshy annual requires some heat for germination; sow seeds in spring under glass in a temperature of 16°C (60°F). Prick off seedlings into a good growing medium, harden off in the usual way and plant out at the end of spring at intervals of 23-30cm (9-12in). Alternatively sow in flowering positions at the end of spring, and thin out to correct distances apart when plants are large enough.

Take care

Remove faded flowers regularly. 104▸

Mesembryanthemum oculatus 'Lunette'

(Livingstone daisy)

- **Sow in spring**
- **Ordinary or poor soil**
- **Sunny position**

The appealing cultivar 'Lunette' is a clear yellow, 8cm (3.2in) high, flowering much earlier than the crinifolium types. Try to plant it near light blue annuals in the border. For formal designs and in window boxes use it along the front edge, or in hanging baskets in a sunny position; in the latter it should be planted before other subjects are included in the design. As the plants are low in height, remember not to plant them too near overpowering species, or they can become smothered.

Spring sowings are essential if this plant is to flower early. Germination will take two or three weeks if kept at a temperature of 18-21°C (65-70°F). Prick off seedlings into a good growing medium, preferably loam-based. Grow on at a lower temperature and then harden off in the usual way. Plant out at the end of spring at 23cm (9in) intervals.

Keep an eye open for slug damage and bait if necessary.

Take care

Do not plant out too early. 104▸

Mimulus guttatus

(Monkey flower)

- **Sow in spring**
- **Ordinary but moist soil**
- **Sunny location or shade**

The yellow flowers, about 2cm (0.8in) long, are trumpet-shaped, and something like those of the snapdragon; small brown dots or blotches in the throat and on the inside of the yellow petals attract many useful insects. The stems, carrying ovate light green leaves, are about 23cm (9in) long. Flowers appear from early summer in most areas.

Moist conditions will give the finest results and these plants are ideal for bog gardens; but they will be quite happy in the ordinary border as long as it is not too hot or too dry.

Treat this plant as a biennial for propagating purposes. Sow seeds in a cold frame in late spring for flowering the following year. Plant out the seedlings in nursery rows in the garden, a few inches apart. Grow on through the summer and keep well watered and weeded, until setting the plants out where they are to flower in early spring.

Take care

Keep moist at all times.

Mimulus variegatus

(Monkey flower)

- **Sow in late winter**
- **Ordinary but moist soil**
- **Sunny position or shade**

Nearly all mimulus plants like a moist site and this species is no exception. They are very useful in the bog garden or as a marginal plant along the edge of a waterside planting. They are also at home as ground cover plants in the shade, as long as ground conditions remain moist throughout the growing period. Open trumpet-shaped flowers are produced on stems 30cm (12in) high. Individual blooms are 5cm (2in) long and can be yellow, orange or scarlet, and blotched with brown, maroon or purple. The supporting leaves are obovate to oblong. Dwarf strains are available, but flowers tend to be the same size.

Sow seed in late winter or very early spring under glass in a temperature of 13°C (55°F). Use any good growing medium of a loam-based nature. Pot seedlings into individual small pots, and grow on in cool conditions. Plant in late spring or early summer at 30cm (12in).

Take care

Avoid hot, dry situations. 105▸

Myosotis alpestris 'Ultramarine'

(Forget-me-not)

- **Sow in late spring**
- **Most soils**
- **Sun or partial shade**

This is strongly recommended for spring bedding, especially in association with wallflowers and tulips. 'Ultramarine' has flowers of a deep indigo blue, produced on very neat compact plants only 15cm (6in) high; the individual flowers are fairly small but have attractive yellow centres. Stems and leaves feel slightly sticky, due to the mass of small hairs. This to some extent has a repellent effect against birds that devastate other spring-flowering plants.

Treat this species as a hardy biennial by sowing seed in nursery beds in late spring. When seedlings are large enough, plant them in further nursery rows, 15cm (6in) apart; grow on through the summer, and keep well weeded until the autumn when final planting in flowering positions should be undertaken at 15cm (6in) intervals. Water in as necessary so that wilting is kept to a minimum.

Take care

Avoid poorly drained soils. 105▸

Nemesia strumosa

- **Sow in early spring**
- **Most soils, but well cultivated**
- **Sunny and slightly moist location**

Nemesia in the wild is rather untidy, but attractive; continued selection and breeding has led to today's more manageable plants. Many self colours are available but I prefer the mixtures that give a wide variety of colours: usually included are shades of yellow, cream, pink, crimson, blue and purple. Individual blooms are 2.5cm (1in) across and funnel-shaped; these are carried on erect branching stems of up to 45cm (18in). The leaves are pale green and coarsely toothed; some change from green to a pinkish red.

This species is very useful as a bedding plant or in window boxes or other containers. Sow seeds under glass in early spring at a temperature of 16°C (60°F). Only just cover the seed, in boxes or pots of a good loam-based growing medium. Harden off slowly and plant out in flowering positions in early summer, at 15cm (6in) apart.

Take care

Make a second sowing one month after the first, for succession. 106-7▸

Nemophila menziesii

(N. insignis)

(Baby blue eyes)

- **Sow in spring**
- **Ordinary but moist soil**
- **Sun or partial shade**

This is one of the more notable hardy annuals from California; plants grow to a height of 23cms (9in), and have spreading slender stems on which deeply cut feathery light green leaves are carried. Appearing from early summer, the flowers are buttercup-shaped and of a beautiful sky blue with a very striking white centre; each bloom measures 4cm (1.6in) in diameter. This species will tolerate partial shade; use it where a low planting is required.

Before sowing, fork in organic matter if your soil is on the light side; this will ensure that moisture is retained in hot dry spells so that plants can survive. Sow seeds directly where they are to flower, in early spring; take out shallow drills and only lightly cover the seed. Thin out seedlings to 15cm (6in) apart. In mild districts autumn sowings carried out in the same way will provide plants for flowering in late spring of the following year.

Take care

Water freely during dry weather. 106▸

Nicandra physaloides

(Shoo fly plant; Apple of Peru)

- **Sow in early spring**
- **Rich well-cultivated soil**
- **Sunny position**

This is a very strong annual, up to 1m (39in) in height. The pale blue bell-shaped flowers, 4cm (1.6in) long, have a contrasting white throat. The flower is followed by a non-edible green apple-shaped fruit encased in a five-winged purple calyx. Stems tend to be branched and spreading; the finely toothed leaves have wavy edges and are a pleasant green. Because of their ultimate size these plants require plenty of room to develop, and they are best used towards the back of an annual or mixed border, preferably in full sun. Before planting, fork in plenty of organic matter.

This unusual annual is easily grown from seed. Sow under glass in early spring at a temperature of 16°C (60°F). Use a good growing medium for sowing and potting. Put seedlings into individual small pots and grow on in the same temperature. Harden off in the usual way and plant out in early summer, 30cm (12in) apart.

Take care

Support individual specimens. 107▸

Nicotiana × sanderae 'Crimson Rock' F1

(Sweet-scented tobacco plant)

- **Sow in early spring**
- **Fertile and well-drained soil**
- **Sun or partial shade**

One of many hybrids now available, 'Crimson Rock' is a beautiful free-flowering compact variety 45cm (18in) high; the blooms are crimson in colour and sweetly fragrant. It has the added advantage that the flowers stay open throughout the day, when other types tend to close.

As with all nicotianas, stems and leaves are sticky to the touch; these usually attract aphids in the early stages of the plant's growth and it is wise to spray them. Because of the very fragrant flowers, grow in beds or borders towards the centre, beneath windows or on patios.

As a half-hardy annual this species needs to be propagated under glass in early spring. Sow seeds on top of prepared pots or boxes of a peat-based growing medium; do not cover the seeds. Keep in a temperature of 18°C (65°F). Prick off seedlings in the usual way. Harden off and plant out in early summer, 23cm (9in) apart.

Take care

Spray early against insects. 108▸

Nicotiana × sanderae 'Nicki Hybrids' F1

(Sweet-scented tobacco plant)

- **Sow in early spring**
- **Rich, well-drained soil**
- **Sun or partial shade**

The Nicki F1 Hybrids are a lovely mixture of colours including red, pink, rose, lime green and white. Individual blooms are up to 6cm (2.4in) long, formed into loose clusters. Stems bearing the flowers carry large oblong leaves of a light green. This strain is dwarf and reaches only about 25cm (10in) in height. The blooms of this free-flowering cultivar are sweetly fragrant. Use as a bedding plant for formal beds or borders, beneath a window, or on a patio or yard where the scent can be appreciated, especially in the evening.

Sow seeds under glass in early spring, in a temperature of 18°C (65°F). Seeds should be scattered thinly on top of prepared pots or boxes of a peat-based growing medium. Prick out in the usual way. Harden off and plant out in early summer, 23cm (9in) apart.

Take care

Do not plant out too early. 108-9▸

Nicotiana tabacum

(N. gigantea)

(Tobacco plant)

- **Sow in early spring**
- **Rich, well-drained soil**
- **Sunny position**

The true tobacco plant can reach a height of 2m (6.5ft) and therefore if you are considering this plant for an ornamental effect in the garden the choice of site will need to be carefully considered. Large leaves up to 1m long are borne on strong stems. Dull red or pink flowers of a funnel shape usually appear from midsummer until autumn. Use these plants in groups at the back of an annual border as an architectural feature, or in large containers on a patio. The leaves will change from green to a light golden colour towards autumn.

Sow under glass in early spring, in a temperature of 18°C (65°F). Use any good growing medium. Prick off into individual small pots and grow on. Give a weak liquid feed up to hardening-off time, about every 10 days. Plant out in early summer at intervals of 60-90cm (2-3ft). A sheltered sunny site will avoid the necessity for staking, especially if plants are grouped together.

Take care

Spray against aphids.

Nigella damascena

(Love-in-a-mist)

- **Sow in early spring**
- **Well-cultivated ordinary soil**
- **Sunny position**

An old favourite, love in a mist is particularly good for the annual border when planted towards the centre. Growing up to 60cm (24in), the stiff stems carry cornflower-like blooms of blue, mauve, purple, rose-pink or white. Bright green feathery foliage gives a light feeling to the plant. The semi-double blooms are followed by the seedpods, much prized for floral arrangements.

Being hardy annuals, these plants are easy to raise, simply by sowing where they are to flower. Rake down to a fine tilth the area to sow, take out shallow drills in early spring, sow the seeds and lightly cover over. When large enough to handle, thin out the seedlings to 23cm (9in) apart. In mild districts autumn sowings made in the same way will produce earlier flowering plants the following year. Discard any unwanted self-sown seedlings at the end of each season.

Take care

Cut stems for drying when seedpods are a light brown. 109◆

Papaver glaucum

(Tulip poppy)

- **Sow in autumn or spring**
- **Ordinary soil**
- **Sunny location**

An annual in habit, this beautiful poppy from Asia Minor has tulip-shaped flowers of four petals, about 10cm (4in) across. Individual flowers are a shining scarlet-crimson. Before opening in early summer they are preceded by pointed buds, carried on blue-green upright stems 45cm (18in) in height. Leaves are deeply cut and similar in colour to the stems.

Use in the annual or mixed border, in bold groups. If used next to a less showy plant, they will stand out even better. The silky texture of the petals will catch the smallest rays of the sun. Plants can be kept flowering longer if seed heads are removed.

As this is a hardy annual, the seeds can be sown in autumn to flower the following year; plants will be stronger and they stand up well to severe winter weather conditions. Spring sowings will make a useful contribution to the border. Sow in shallow drills and cover lightly. Thin out seedlings to 30cm (12in).

Take care

Water freely during dry weather.

Papaver rhoeas

(Corn poppy)

- **Sow in autumn or spring**
- **Light well-drained soil**
- **Sunny location**

From the common wild scarlet field poppy the Rev. W. Wilks made his famous selections from which, in the 1880s, the world-renowned Shirley poppy strain was introduced. Mainly in the range of pink, red and white, a number will be found to be bicoloured or picotee. Double strains now exist, but the single type are more allied to the original introductions. This very worthy annual is hardy, and can be used in borders and in the odd pocket towards the back of a rock garden, as long as the position is sunny.

Up to 60cm (24in) in height, the stems carry lovely deeply lobed leaves above which the flowers are borne, about 7.5cm (3in) across.

Sow seeds in spring or autumn. Take out shallow drills where the plants are to flower. Sow seeds and lightly cover with soil. Thin out seedlings to 30cm (12in) apart. Flowers appear in early summer.

Take care

Spray against aphids.

Papaver somniferum 'Paeony-flowered Mixed'

(Opium poppy)

- **Sow in spring or autumn**
- **Ordinary soil**
- **Sunny position**

The large paeony-flowered mixture and is well recommended for the garden. Individual double flowers measure up to 10cm (4in) across. Blue-green deeply lobed leaves are carried on smooth stems 75cm (30in) tall. Pink, white, red or purple blooms will appear in early summer and although relatively short-lived they are worth a place in the annual border. The flowers are followed by large bulbous seedpods much prized by flower arrangers.

These poppies are easily grown from seeds sown in the autumn in mild districts, or in the spring elsewhere. Take out drills large enough for the seeds, about 30cm (12in) apart. Cover the seeds lightly with soil; thin out the seedlings to 30cm (12in) apart. Although fairly tall, these plants should not require staking. In severe winters protect autumn-sown seedlings from the weather.

Take care

Spray against mildew disease. 110▸

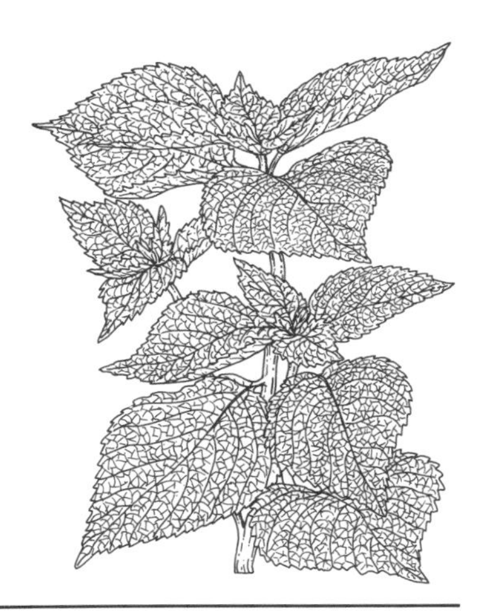

Pelargonium zonale

(Geranium)

- **Sow in winter or very early spring**
- **Ordinary well-drained soil**
- **Full sun**

Zonal geraniums have become increasingly popular in recent years, and many new seed-raised cultivars have been introduced. F1 hybrids will begin to flower at bedding-out time if sown in heat under glass in early spring. Their well-formed florets of single flowers are borne in large trusses; the few new double kinds are slightly later flowering. Foliage may be plain or with darker zones, and there are several interesting dwarf hybrids.

Geraniums grow in ordinary soil provided they receive sunshine. Sow thinly in seed mixture in a temperature of 21-24°C (70-75°F), just covering the seed. Germination may take three weeks. Prick off singly into small pots when large enough, and grow on in a lower temperature until ready for planting out in a sunny position after frosts are past.

Take care

Remove dead flowerheads to prevent seeding.

Perilla nankinensis

(P. frutescens)

- **Sow in very early spring**
- **Ordinary well-cultivated soil**
- **Sunny site**

Grown for its beautiful bronze-purple foliage, this half-hardy annual is most useful as a spot plant in formal bedding schemes or as an architectural plant in the mixed or annual border. If you have a patio surrounded by a light-coloured wall, large containers of this plant will provide a unique contrast.

The showy leaves are toothed, ovate and pointed. When bruised, these and the insignificant white flowers emit a spice-like fragrance, reminiscent of their Chinese origin. Given good conditions, plants reach a height of 60cm (24in).

Propagate under glass in very early spring. Sow seeds in pots or boxes of a good growing medium. Keep in a temperature of 18°C (65°F). Prick off the seedlings into individual pots. Harden off and plant out in early summer. If growing together in groups allow 30cm (12in) between plants.

Take care

Stake individual specimens. 111▸

Petunia hybrids

- **Sow in early spring**
- **Ordinary well-cultivated soil**
- **Sunny location**

In a good sunny summer the petunia is second to none for its profusion of colour and versatility of use. Flowers are trumpet-shaped, up to 10cm (4in) across. Leaves and stems will be a mid- to dark green; leaves vary in size but are usually ovate. The whole plant feels sticky to the touch. Use these petunias for a wide range of purposes including formal bedding, borders, containers, window boxes and hanging baskets.

All petunias love a sunny position and benefit from being grown in a well-cultivated soil. Avoid having the soil over-rich, as this can lead to a lot of growth and few flowers. As this is a tender annual, seeds will need to be sown under glass in early spring. Sow thinly on top of a peat-based growing medium in pots or boxes. Prick off the seedlings into boxes, harden off and plant out in early summer. Spacing will depend on the cultivar you choose.

Take care

Remove faded flowers regularly. 110▸

Phacelia campanularia

- **Sow in early spring**
- **Light, sandy, well-drained soil**
- **Sunny site**

This is one of the most striking annuals. The gentian-blue clusters of upturned bell-shaped flowers are worth a place in any annual border. Blooms appear from early summer. Each individual flower has lovely contrasting pale yellow stamens; overall, blooms are about 2.5cm (1in) across. Plants are dwarf and branching in character, about 23cm (9in) high. Stems carry ovate leaves that are cut or toothed along the edge, and dark greyish green in colour. Loved by bees, these plants are ideally suited to the edge of a border or pathway, preferably planted in bold groups to make a greater impact.

In early spring rake down the soil to a fine tilth, sow the seeds thinly in shallow drills where they are to flower and cover lightly. Thin out the subsequent seedlings to 15cm (6in) apart. If your garden is in a relatively mild area, then seeds can be sown in autumn. Plants grown through the winter will flower somewhat earlier.

Take care

Watch out for slugs. 112▸

Phlox drummondii 'Carnival'

- **Sow in spring**
- **Ordinary well-drained soil**
- **Open, sunny site**

Easy-to-grow half-hardy annuals, *P. drummondii* will give a succession of colour throughout the summer. For a really bright display try the cultivar 'Carnival'; this mixture has pink, rose, salmon, scarlet, blue and violet flowers. These are borne on stems 30cm (12in) high, carrying light green lanceolate leaves. Blooms are produced in early summer as dense heads up to 10cm (4in) in diameter; each individual flower is rounded. These plants are ideally suited for low-growing areas of the garden, especially the rock garden, where pockets can be filled to give constant colour.

In spring, sow seeds under glass in a temperature of 16°C (60°F). Use any good growing medium for sowing. Sow the seeds thinly and cover them lightly. Prick off the young seedlings, when large enough to handle, into boxes or trays. Harden off and plant out in flowering positions in early summer at 23cm (9in) intervals.

Take care
Dead-head to prolong flowering. 129▸

Portulaca grandiflora

(Sun plant)

- **Sow in spring**
- **Ordinary well-drained soil**
- **Full sun**

Originating from Brazil, portulacas have now come into their own as worthwhile plants for the annual border or (more especially) for pockets in the rock garden. In some areas they can be temperamental but given a good sunny site they should thrive well on most soils. The flowers of *P. grandiflora* are produced on semi-prostrate stems of a reddish colour, usually up to 23cm (9in) in height. Red, purple, rose, orange-scarlet, yellow and white, the blooms can be over 2.5cm (1in) across. Each centre has pronounced yellow stamens. Leaves are narrow, round and fleshy.

Sow seed in early spring under glass, in a temperature of 18°C (65°F). Use any good growing medium for this purpose and for the subsequent pricking-off of seedlings. Harden off in a cold frame and plant out in early summer, 15cm (6in) apart. Alternatively, sow where they are to flower, in mid-spring.

Take care
Water established plants only in extreme temperatures. 129▸

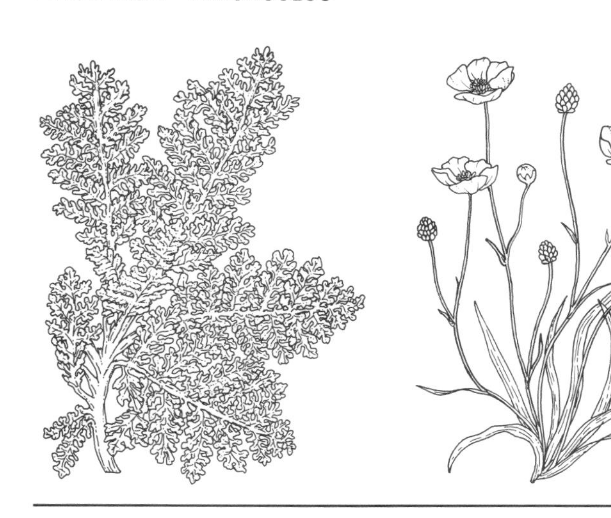

Pyrethrum ptarmicaeflorum 'Silver Feathers'

(P. roseum)

- **Sow in early spring**
- **Light, well-drained soil**
- **Sunny position**

This is a fine plant used extensively for its silver-grey foliage. The lacy leaves are borne on slender 30cm (12in) stems. The cultivar 'Silver Feathers' is particularly elegant. Although this species is strictly a perennial, plants are raised from seed each year as annuals. Besides using them as an edging plant, group three or five together as spot plants in a small bed with *Begonia semperflorens* as the predominant plant. Make sure that areas to be planted with this plant are very well drained; provide extra drainage by forking in coarse washed sand.

Raise plants by sowing seeds in early spring under glass, in a temperature of 16°C (60°F). Sow thinly in pots and only just cover the seeds. Use any good growing medium. Prick off seedlings and harden off in the usual way. Plant out 15cm (6in) apart.

Take care

Remove flowers regularly to keep foliage neat. 130▸

Ranunculus gramineus

- **Sow in early spring**
- **Ordinary soil**
- **Sun or partial shade**

One of a great number of species of the buttercup family *R. gramineus* is an extremely valuable plant to have in the garden. Buttercup flowers are produced in sprays on 30cm (12in) stems. The leaves are grey-green and grass-like. Appearing from late spring to midsummer, the yellow blooms are 2cm (0.8in) in diameter, shiny in texture and very free flowering. Mainly used in drifts in slightly moist areas, these plants will also give a good account of themselves in most borders, especially in conjunction with annual grasses or the blue linums.

Raise plants each year from seed by sowing in a frame or under cloches. Sow directly into the ground during early spring in shallow drills. Thin out the seedlings and remove the frame top or cloche in mid-spring. Grow on until autumn, then plant in final flowering positions.

Take care

Keep young plants cool through the summer months. 130▸

Reseda odorata

(Mignonette)

- **Sow in early spring or autumn**
- **Most soils except very acid ones**
- **Sunny location**

Having a very distinctive sweet scent, mignonette has long been a favourite. Flowers are carried on branching upright stems 75cm (30in) in height. Individual flowers are made up of very small petals in the centre of which is a mass of orange tufted stamens; clusters of these blooms are formed into a loose head. Leaves are a light green and spathe-shaped, smooth and terminating just below the blooms. Planted towards the back of a border mignonette will look and smell fine.

Sow seeds where they are to flower, in early spring or autumn. Take out drills and lightly cover the seed. To assist germination and better-shaped plants, firm the soil well after sowing, either with the back of the rake or by treading lightly with your feet. Thin out subsequent seedlings to 15-23cm (6-9in) apart. Flowers will appear from early summer onwards.

Take care

Do not overwater mature plants. 131▸

Ricinus communis

(Castor oil plant)

- **Sow in early spring**
- **Ordinary well-cultivated soil**
- **Sunny location**

Treated as a half-hardy annual for normal garden work, this species originates from Africa.

Grown for the beautiful large palmate leaves up to 30cm (12in) across, castor oil plants are best used at the back of an informal border to give height and character. Depending on the cultivar the leaves will be green, purple or bronze. Petal-less flowers are produced in summer, followed by large spiky round seedpods; these can be poisonous if the internal seeds are eaten.

Sow seeds in early spring in a heated greenhouse at a temperature of 21°C (70°F). Sow in individual pots of a good growing medium. Move on into larger pots (10cm/4in), and reduce the temperature to 10°C (50°F). Harden off the plants in a cold frame at least two weeks before planting out in early summer.

Take care

Staking will be necessary. 132▸

Rudbeckia hirta 'Marmalade'

(Black-eyed Susan; Cone flower)

- **Sow in spring**
- **Any soil**
- **Sunny position**

The common names of this species allude to the centre of the flower, which has a very dark brown to purple colour and is cone-shaped. The outer petals are lovely shades of yellow, golds and brown, and the cultivar 'Marmalade' is a rich yellow with a central cone of purple-black – very striking. It flowers from early summer, and blooms will be carried in great profusion until late autumn on stems 45cm (18in) long. Individual flowers will be up to 10cm (4in) across.

To obtain flowering plants each year, sow seeds in boxes of any good growing medium in spring. Heat will not be required and they can be raised in either a cold greenhouse or a frame. Prick out the young seedlings into boxes and place these in a cold frame to protect them from frosts. Harden off in late spring and plant out into flowering positions in very early summer, 23cm (9in) apart.

Take care

Watch out for slug damage. 132▸

Salpiglossis sinuata 'Grandiflora'

- **Sow in very early spring**
- **Ordinary but well-cultivated soil**
- **Open and sunny position**

Although usually grown as a pot plant this species is a worthwhile subject to use outdoors in the summer months as a bedding plant.

'Grandiflora' and its hybrids will provide a wealth of colour in shades of crimson, scarlet, gold, rose, blue and yellow. Each flower has a velvet texture and the throat of the tubular flowers is often deeply veined with a contrasting colour. Size of individual blooms will vary between named cultivars of the species but they are on average about 5cm (2in) long and the same in diameter. Up to 60cm (24in) in height, the stems are slender and carry wavy-edged narrow leaves of a dark green.

Sow seed under glass in very early spring to produce plants for growing outdoors in summer. Use a peat-based growing medium for raising the seed, and keep in a temperature of 18°C (65°F). Prick out seedlings into boxes, harden off and plant out in early summer, 23cm (9in) apart.

Take care

Keep well watered at all times. 133▸

Above: **Phlox drummondii 'Carnival'**
This sweetly scented dwarf mixture includes many lovely colours with contrasting eyes. 125▸

Below: **Portulaca grandiflora**
In dry sunny situations these fleshy leaved plants will abound with bright flowers during the summer. Water established plants sparingly. 125▸

Above: **Pyrethrum ptarmicaeflorum 'Silver Feathers'**
The elegant silver-grey foliage of this plant makes it ideal for edging. Raise new plants from seed each year. 126▸

Left: **Ranunculus gramineus**
For masses of yellow flowers in late spring plant this dwarf buttercup in generous drifts in the border. Will tolerate partial shade. 126▸

Right: **Reseda odorata**
An established favourite, this plant deserves to be widely grown for its sweet scent alone. Ideal for the back of the border. 127▸

Above: **Ricinus communis**
These stately plants add height and interest to the border. Plant in early summer and provide support. 127▸

Below: **Rudbeckia hirta 'Marmalade'**
These long-lasting golden flowers are borne on tall stems. 128▸

Above: **Salpiglossis sinuata 'Grandiflora'**
Velvety textured, multicoloured flowers are borne on stems up to 60cm (24in) in height. A fine summer bedding plant that can be cut. 128▸

Left: **Salvia horminum**
The striking blue or purple bracts surround the true flowers, which are insignificant. Grow these attractive plants in well-drained soil in a sunny location for best results. 145▸

Right: **Salvia sclarea**
This is a useful plant for a large border, both for its bold foliage and for its elegant sprays of true flowers and showy bracts. Grow this biennial in sun on light soil. 146▸

Below: **Salvia splendens 'Flarepath'**
The bright scarlet spikes of true flowers and bracts make a vivid contrast against the dark green foliage of these well-loved plants. Superbly showy for formal beds, containers and window boxes. 147▸

Left: **Sanvitalia procumbens**
These miniature flowers are borne on branching stems that reach only 15cm (6in) high. Ideal as an edging and ground cover plant, it will thrive in an open sunny position. 147▶

Right: **Schizanthus pinnatus 'Angel Wings'**
Delicate butterfly flowers float above the fine feathery foliage. This free-flowering cultivar grows 30cm (12in) high and does not need staking. Suitable for containers. 148▶

Below: **Silybum marianum**
Grow these striking plants at the back of the border, where their bold green leaves flecked with white will add height and interest. Thistle flowers in late summer. 148▶

Left: **Thunbergia alata**
This vigorous annual climber will grow well outdoors in a sunny and sheltered spot. The pretty flowers are freely produced throughout the summer. Provide support. 151▸

Right: **Tropaeolum peregrinum**
Also a climber, this colourful plant will quickly spread over a fence or trellis, producing masses of lovely fringed flowers in summer. Feeding will give leaves, not flowers. 152▸

Below: **Tagetes erecta 'Orange Jubilee' F1**
This fine marigold holds its large flowerheads well above the dense foliage. The lovely blooms are double and will last well if cut. 149▸

Above: **Ursinia anethoides 'Sunshine'**
Bright golden yellow flowers that need sunshine to open fully. 153▸

Below: **Venidium fastuosum**
Stunning blooms up to 10cm (4in) across are borne on tall stems. Excellent as cut flowers indoors. 153▸

Above:
Verbascum bombyciferum
Bold architectural plants. Flowering stems reach a height of about 120cm (48in) and bear masses of yellow blooms. Give them room. 154▶

Above: **Verbena 'Florist Mixed'**
A bright mixture with a wide range of colours, many showing contrasting eyes. Grow this dwarf verbena on the rock garden, border edges, and in containers and window boxes. 155▶

Above: **Viola x wittrockiana Swiss Giant type**
This is one of the many varieties of garden pansy available. The colourful flowers are produced over a long period in the summer. 156▸

Below: **Viola cornuta**
This miniature viola is quite hardy and will flower continuously in the summer. In a moist fertile soil it will be equally happy in sun or in partial shade. Ideal for rock gardens. 155▸

Above: **Viscaria elegans 'Love'**
Sow these pretty annuals where they are to flower for a colourful, early summer display in the border. 156▸

Below: **Zinnia elegans 'Hobgoblin Mixed'**
A bright mixture of medium-sized, weather-resistant double flowers. 158▸

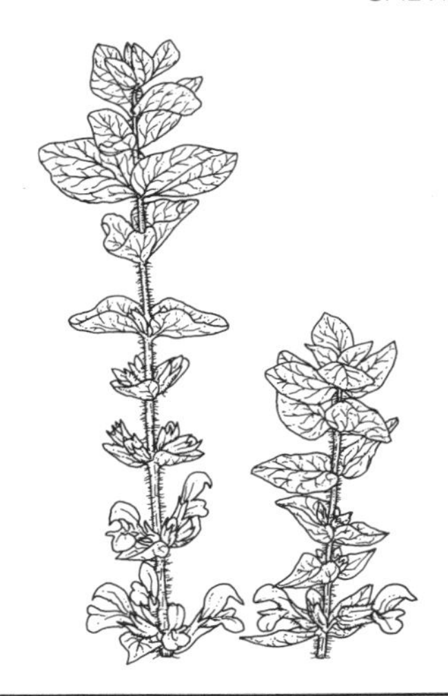

Salvia coccinea

- **Sow in early spring**
- **Ordinary soil**
- **Sunny position**

Often confused with *S. splendens* because of their close resemblance, *S. coccinea* has slightly longer flowers and is more slender in habit. Growing to 60cm (24in) it is more suited to the mixed or herbaceous border than for formal planting in beds. Deep scarlet tubular flowers show colour later than those of its more popular cousin, usually about midsummer onwards. Leaves are cordate or ovate, hairy and a lightish green. The species is variable and a number of sub-species are available, such as 'bicolor', 'lactea' and 'nana', all excellent for specific purposes.

S. coccinea should be grown from seed each year during early spring. Sow seeds in a peat-based growing medium under glass, in a temperature of 18°C (65°F). Prick off the seedlings singly into individual peat pots; in this way stronger plants will be obtained. Grow on in a reduced temperature. Harden off and plant out in early summer at 30cm (12in) intervals.

Take care
Check for slug or snail damage.

Salvia horminum

(Clary)

- **Sow in early spring or autumn**
- **Ordinary well-drained soil**
- **Sunny position**

This salvia from S Europe will provide a completely different range of colour from the *S. splendens* scarlet cultivars. Dark blue or purple bracts are produced around the insignificant true flowers. Mixtures are available, but the cultivar 'Blue Beard' is recommended for its very deep purple bracts on erect branching square stems, 45cm (18in) high. These also carry the ovate mid-green leaves. Grow towards the front of a border, or as a formal bedding plant with a few silver spot plants.

These hardy annuals may be sown direct outdoors in spring or autumn. If earlier colour is required plants can be raised under glass by sowing in seed mixture in spring at a temperature of 18°C (65°F). Prick off into individual pots or seed trays. Grow on cooler and harden off to plant out at 23cm (9in) apart in early summer. Too high temperatures will produce soft elongated growth.

Take care
Thin seedlings sown outdoors before they become crowded. 134▸

Salvia patens

- **Sow in early spring**
- **Ordinary soil**
- **Sunny spot**

Another species of the useful sage family, *S. patens* originates from Mexico. When plants are in flower the vivid blue colour is probably the best of its shade in the summer months. Individual blooms will be 5cm (2in) long, tubular in shape, consisting of lower and upper joined lips. Up to 45cm (18in) in height, the plants have sage-like leaves that are ovate and pointed, of a lovely green; the stiff stems are square. Although these plants are half-hardy perennials, they are usually treated as annuals for most purposes.

Sow seeds in very early spring in a warm greenhouse, keeping a constant temperature of 18°C (65°F). Use any good growing medium for seed raising and pricking out. The latter should be done into individual small pots. Grow on until hardening off in early summer. Plant out into final positions, 30cm (12in) apart.

Take care
Pinch out tips of young plants for bushy growth.

Salvia sclarea

(Clary)

- **Sow in spring**
- **Light and fertile soil**
- **Full sun**

This handsome biennial was grown in the past for use as a culinary herb but is now surpassed by the various species of sage. The oil, however, is still extracted commercially for use in the manufacture of perfumes. Reaching a height of 75cm (30in), the stems carry large, very hairy triangular leaves of mid-green. Flowers are tubular in shape, about 2.5cm (1in) long, and white-blue in colour. Below the true flowers, bracts of purple or yellow will accentuate the whole blooms, which show colour from midsummer onward. These are good border plants, which will enhance an otherwise flat area; use them towards the back of the border.

This species is biennial in habit. The seeds are sown in spring where they are to flower. Take out drills 38cm (15in) apart; thin out seedlings to 30cm (12in) apart when they are large enough to handle.

Take care
Use leaves for culinary purposes from midsummer onwards. 135▸

Salvia splendens 'Flarepath'

(Scarlet sage)

- **Sow in early spring**
- **Ordinary well-drained soil**
- **Sunny position**

Of all summer annuals the scarlet flowers (actually, bracts) of *S. splendens* must be the most vivid. Planted in formal beds or borders with contrasting silver- or grey-leaved plants they provide a stunning spectacle. Of the many cultivars available 'Flarepath' is well recommended and enjoys great popularity. The flowers are produced on 30cm (12in) stems above the rich green ovate leaves; they usually start to appear in early summer.

This tender plant requires a greenhouse for propagation. Sow seed in early spring in a peat-based growing compost. Keep the temperature about 18°C (65°F). Prick out seedlings into individual small pots and grow on in a slightly lower temperature. Harden off and plant out in summer about 23cm (9in) apart after late frosts are over.

Take care

Provide ample moisture when the plants are established. 135▸

Sanvitalia procumbens

(Creeping zinnia)

- **Sow in spring**
- **Ordinary soil**
- **Sunny site**

Very aptly named, the zinnia-like flowers of this hardy annual are quite striking. Bright yellow single flowers have jet black cone centres. They are 2.5cm (1in) across, produced on semi-prostrate branching stems only 15cm (6in) high from early summer onwards. Leaves are ovate, pointed and a useful green.

For successful results, fork peat or other humus into the top layer of soil before sowing the seed. To have plants flowering through the summer months, sow seeds outdoors in spring or earlier under glass; the latter will produce stronger, earlier-flowering specimens. Take out shallow drills where the plants are to flower, and lightly cover the seed with soil. Thin out the spring-sown seedlings as soon as they are large enough to handle; those sown in heat should be hardened off for later planting. In either case, thin out to 7.5cm (3in) apart.

Take care

Keep well watered if in hanging baskets. 136▸

Schizanthus pinnatus 'Angel wings'

(Butterfly flower)

- **Sow in spring**
- **Ordinary well-drained soil**
- **Sunny position**

The very tall cultivars of this spec'es are now being replaced by more manageable dwarfer forms for garden work. Use them as border plants or even in formal bedding. 'Angel Wings' is a cultivar well worth trying for all purposes. Only 30cm (12in) tall the plants are very free-flowering, compact and almost conical in shape, and will not require staking. Flowers are orchid-shaped and come in a wide variety of colours; the spotted petals and open throats of the blooms are most attractive. Stems and leaves are a light green, the latter being deeply cut and fern-like.

As this is a half-hardy annual, sow seeds under glass in spring at a temperature of 16°C (60°F). Use a peat-based growing medium for sowing and for the subsequent pricking-off of seedlings. Harden off and plant out into flowering positions in early summer, 23cm (9in) apart.

Take care

Avoid watering overhead in very hot weather. 137▸

Silybum marianum

(Our Lady's milk thistle)

- **Sow in spring or autumn**
- **Any soil**
- **Sunny and open site**

Beautiful thistle flowers of a violet colour are produced in late summer by this lovely plant from the Mediterranean. More often than not, though, it is grown for its remarkable foliage; the attractive dark green leaves are mottled or flecked with white. Ovate in shape, they carry spines in and around the lobes. Stems carrying the flowers can be up to 1.5m (5ft) in height and arise from rosettes of the beautiful glossy leaves. Use this as an architectural plant at the back of a mixed, annual or herbaceous border.

Stronger plants will be obtained if seed is sown in autumn rather than in the spring. In either case take out drills where the plants are to be effective. Sow the seed and lightly cover over. Thin out the young seedlings as early as possible, to 60cm (24in) apart. Despite their height these plants should not require staking, and it should be avoided, or the effect can be spoiled.

Take care

Give plants enough space. 136▸

Tagetes erecta 'Orange Jubilee' F1

(African marigold)

- **Sow in spring**
- **Any soil**
- **Open and sunny site**

Nearly all marigolds are very reliable, and the cultivar 'Orange Jubilee' is no exception. One of a strain of Jubilee types growing to 60cm (24in) tall, they are often referred to as 'hedge forms' because of the dense foliage. 'Orange Jubilee' is an F1 Hybrid and although seeds are relatively expensive they are worth the extra cost because of the reliable uniformity of flower. Carnation-shaped double blooms are produced on the almost erect stems of very sturdy plants; light orange in colour, individual flowers can be 10cm (4in) in diameter. Foliage, kept below the flowers, is light green and deeply cut. All parts of the plant are very pungent. This cultivar can be used for nearly all purposes. The plants will look well formally planted with other complementary subjects.

Raise young plants as other *Tagetes* described here. Plant out 'Orange Jubilee' at 30cm (12in) apart.

Take care

Dead-head to prolong flowering. 138▸

Tagetes patula 'Yellow Jacket'

(French marigold)

- **Sow in spring**
- **Ordinary, even poor soil**
- **Open and sunny site**

Few annuals provide such good value as the marigolds. They tolerate most conditions except shade, and even on poor soils they do remarkably well. Continual dead-heading of plants will give a longer flowering season. Recent introductions – and there have been many–can make it difficult to choose, but 'Yellow Jacket' is strongly recommended for its dwarfness. Only 15cm (6in) in height, it has large double carnation-like flowers of bright yellow, which shine in warm sunny conditions; they are also slightly crested. These lovely flowers are formed on very compact plants carrying dark deeply cut leaves.

Sow under glass in spring. Use any good growing medium to raise the seed. Keep in a temperature of 18°C (65°F). Prick off the young seedlings in the usual way. Harden off and plant out in early summer, 15cm (6in) apart, after the risk of frost.

Take care

Spray against aphid attacks. 8▸

Tagetes patula 'Florence'

- **Sow in spring**
- **Ordinary soil**
- **Open and sunny site**

For many years, crosses have been made between the French and African marigolds, resulting in 'hybrida' strains. 'Florence' is a cultivar of this type and is well recommended for garden use. Single, orange-gold flowers 6cm (2.4in) across are produced on 50cm (20in) branching erect stems; these also carry lovely light green finely cut foliage. The bushy compact plants will provide early and continuous flowers from early summer onwards. For a good display near the house, plant them in containers in late spring; otherwise use them in beds or borders with suitable annuals of a contrasting colour, planting out in early summer. Make sure the site is open and sunny. Enrich the soil with humus before planting out.

Sow seed under glass in the usual way, during spring. Keep in a temperature of 18°C (65°F). Harden off and plant out in summer, at 25cm (10in) intervals.

Take care

Dead-head to prolong flowering.

Tagetes patula 'Silvia'

(Dwarf French marigold)

- **Sow in spring**
- **Most ordinary soil**
- **Sunny position**

Rather a misnomer, the French marigold originates from Mexico. The number of cultivars to choose from increases each year; the recent introduction of 'Silvia' is a dwarf form of the species, growing only 20cm (8in) high. The large yellow blooms are remarkably resistant to unfavourable weather conditions. These compact plants are ideal subjects for edging around formal beds and borders. They are also very useful for the front of window boxes and other containers on a patio or yard. In such conditions water well.

As half-hardy annuals, tagetes need to be raised under glass. Sow seed in spring, in pots or boxes of any good growing medium. Keep in a temperature of 18°C (65°F). Germination is usually very quick, and pricking out should be done as soon as the young seedlings are manageable. Harden off and plant out in early summer, at 23cm (9in).

Take care

Keep established plants on the dry side unless in containers.

Tagetes signata pumila 'Starfire'

(T. tenuifolia)

- **Sow in spring**
- **Ordinary well-cultivated soil**
- **Open sunny location**

These marigolds are noted for their continuous flowering. The dwarf 23cm (9in) plants thrive in sunny positions. This new mixture includes colours from lemon to yellow, orange-brown and mahogany, with many different markings. The finely divided light green leaves are pleasantly scented.

Seeds may be sown in seed mixture under glass from early spring in a temperature of 16-18°C (60-65°F) and lightly covered until germination, which should take about one week. Prick off into trays and grow on in a lower temperature until ready for hardening off; plant out in early summer after danger of frost is past. Space plants about 20cm (8in) apart.

Take care

Overwatering and overfeeding result in too much foliage.

Thunbergia alata

(Clock vine; Black-eyed Susan)

- **Sow in spring**
- **Ordinary, well-drained soil**
- **Sunny and sheltered position**

Surely one of the finest annual climbers, the clock vine comes from S Africa. It freely produces 5cm (2in) wide tubular flowers of orange-yellow, the centre of the tube being dark purple-brown. Blooms are formed from the axils of the ovate light green leaves, which are carried on twining stems up to 3m (10ft) long. This is an ideal climbing plant for the cool greenhouse. If given a sheltered sunny site it will do equally well in the garden: grow it against a south-facing wall, or on tall peasticks in an annual or mixed border. If space and position allow, let this species twine amongst a blue clematis – a lovely combination.

Sow seeds in spring under glass in a temperature of 16-18°C (60-65°F): use any good growing medium. Prick off the seedlings singly into individual small pots and place a split cane in each to give support. Plant out after hardening off in summer.

Take care

Keep young plants well spaced under glass to prevent tangling. 138▸

Tropaeolum majus 'Whirlybird'

(Nasturtium)
- **Sow in spring**
- **Poor soil**
- **Sunny position**

Many of the old cultivars have been superseded by modern forms, a number of which are less vigorous and rambling; 'Whirlybird' mixture is one of these. The short trumpet-shaped flowers lack the usual spur associated with these flowers, and the semi-double blooms face upwards above the foliage. Reaching an ultimate height of 23cm (9in), this cultivar has smooth light green circular leaves. This lovely foil enhances the cherry-rose, gold, mahogany, orange, scarlet or tangerine flowers.

To flower on the border, plant seeds in spring, two seeds per station, 2.5cm (1in) deep. Space seeds at 15cm (6in) intervals. To grow as young plants for planting out in early summer, sow seeds in pots, either one or two seeds per pot. Use a growing medium without nutrients. Keep in a temperature of 13°C (55°F). Plant into flowering positions after hardening off, in early summer.

Take care

Spray against blackfly. 9▸

Tropaeolum peregrinum (T. canariense)

(Canary creeper)
- **Sow in spring**
- **Average soil**
- **Sun or partial shade**

This choice climber, related to the nasturtium, is well worth a place in the garden if you have a suitable site. Strictly short-lived perennials they are treated as annuals for cultivation purposes. The elegantly fringed yellow flowers, 2.5cm (1in) across, have graceful green spurs, and are produced freely from thin twining stems that can reach a height of 4m (13ft) in a single season. Peltate leaves of five lobes, and green-blue in colour, are carried on the full length of the stems. This species is useful over trellis work or on wires.

Sow seeds in early spring to produce flowering plants in the summer. Use any good growing medium, plant two seeds per pot, and keep in a temperature of 13°C (55°F). Place a split cane in each pot to provide support; plant out in early summer, after hardening off.

Take care

Avoid overwatering and do not feed: otherwise plants will make leaves but very few flowers. 139▸

Ursinia anethoides 'Sunshine'

- **Sow in spring**
- **Ordinary or dry soil**
- **Sunny location**

Blooms are daisy-like and come in shades of golden-yellow or orange; often they are banded towards the base of each flower in a striking black or maroon, the central base being in similar colours. Individual blooms will be up to 5cm (2in) across. Stems are 30cm (12in) in height, with finely cut leaves of a light green.

It is very important to plant ursinias in full sunshine, because they tend to close their flowers in dull weather and at night. Make bold plantings of this attractive annual on borders or in formal beds. Useful as a pot plant, they will be quite happy planted into various containers for the yard or patio, as long as the site is sunny.

Sow seeds under glass in spring, and keep a constant temperature of 16°C (60°F). Use any good growing medium that is free draining. Prick off the seedlings into boxes. Harden off in late spring and plant out into flowering positions in early summer, 23cm (9in) apart.

Take care

Add sand to heavy soils. 140▸

Venidium fastuosum

(Monarch of the veldt)

- **Sow in spring**
- **Light, well-drained soil**
- **Sunny position**

As its common name implies, this species originates from S Africa. Up to 60cm (24in) in height, the stems carry terminal blooms of a rich orange, 10cm (4in) in diameter. The petals are banded towards the bottom of each flower in shades of purple-brown. The central cone or disc is black. This striking contrast has no real equal among the summer-flowering annuals. The stems and deeply lobed leaves are often a silver-white texture, giving a woolly effect; this highlights the flowers even more. These plants are excellent for borders when planted in bold drifts, or they can be used for containers. The cut flowers last well.

Sow seeds in spring under glass, in a temperature of 16°C (60°F). Use any good growing medium, and prick out and harden off in the usual way: Plant out in early summer, 30cm (12in) apart. Alternatively, sow seeds where they are to flower, in mid-spring.

Take care

Support with bushy peasticks. 140▸

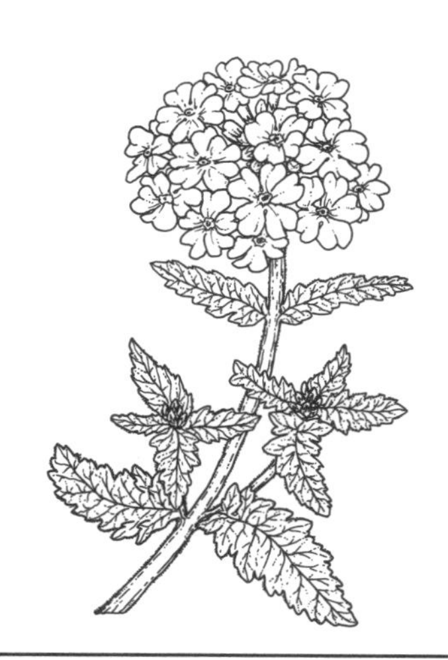

Verbascum bombyciferum

(Mullein)

- **Sow in late spring**
- **Ordinary well-drained soil**
- **Full sun**

Borders often lack plants of good height, colour and architectural effect for the back, but this species of mullein will meet most of those requirements even when not in full flower. Up to 1.3m (4ft) in height, the stems arise from a rosette of large ovate pointed leaves, which have a fine felty texture made up of masses of white-silver hairs. Stems are very erect, and bear a profusion of sulphur-yellow flowers. These are saucer-shaped, up to 5cm (2in) across, with pronounced stamens.

As this is a biennial, seeds will need to be sown in late spring to ensure good flowering plants in the following year. Sow in boxes or pots of any good growing medium, and place in a cold frame. Once germinated, plant out into nursery rows, 20cm (8in) apart. Keep watered and weeded through the summer. Plant out in early autumn, 45-60cm (18-24in) apart.

Take care

Stakes plants in windy sites. 141▶

Verbena × hybrida 'Dwarf Compact Blaze'

(Vervain)

- **Sow in early spring**
- **Ordinary but fertile soil**
- **Sunny location**

Only 18cm (7in) high, this dwarf cultivar is a very useful addition to the general group of verbenas. Plants can provide colour in a small garden without taking up too much precious space; try them beneath half or full standard fuchsias. The vivid scarlet flowers are produced on stems carrying dark green leaves. Plants are free-flowering from early summer until well into the autumn. The compact plants are better raised each year from seed, rather than by the old method of taking cuttings at the end of each flowering season.

Sow seeds in early spring under glass, in a temperature of 18-21°C (65-70°F). Use any good growing medium that is free draining. Germination may be slow so do not be tempted to overwater. Prick off the seedlings into boxes, and harden off in the usual way. Plant out in early summer, 23cm (9in) apart.

Take care

Water freely in very dry conditions, especially on light soils.

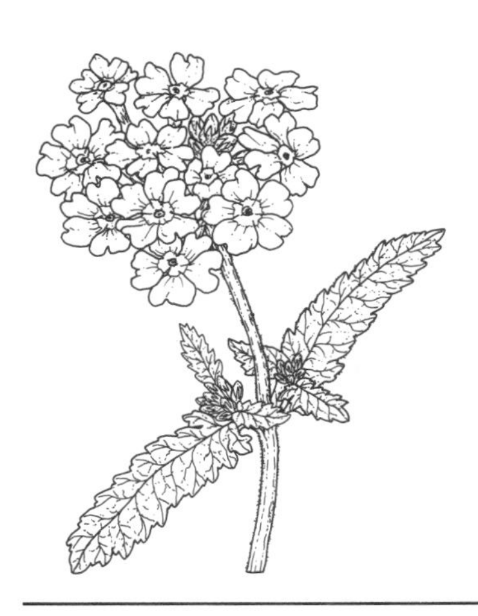

Verbena × hybrida 'Florist Mixed'

(Vervain)

- **Sow in early spring**
- **Any fertile soil**
- **Sunny position**

Another dwarf form of verbena, 'Florist Mixed' provides a diverse colour range. The stems, 23cm (9in) in height, tend to spread and make a mat. The rainbow shades of the flowers are produced above the foliage, which is dark green, and this gives a jewel-like effect. This cultivar is very useful as a front plant for window boxes, the edge of containers, or flower beds and borders. Small pockets on the rock garden make ideal sites.

Sow seeds in pots or boxes in early spring under glass. Keep at a temperature of 16°C (60°F). Use any good growing medium. Prick off the young seedlings as soon as they are ready, into boxes or trays. Harden off and plant out into flowering positions in early summer. Those for containers and window boxes can be planted out slightly earlier as long as they are in sheltered positions. Spacing should be 23cm (9in) apart.

Take care

Water freely in very dry weather. 142▸

Viola cornuta

- **Sow in early spring**
- **Fertile and moist but well-drained soil**
- **Sun or partial shade**

This comes from the Pyrenees and is therefore quite hardy for most garden purposes. The species is usually represented by the lovely lavender- or violet-coloured flowers, although there is the white form 'Alba'. Blooms are angular, and about 2.5cm (1in) across, carried on semi-prostrate soft stems not much longer than 30cm (12in). Leaves are oval to ovate, and green. Use them as an early or midsummer annual for the edge of a border or bed and for the odd pocket in the rock garden. They will tolerate dappled shade as long as the soil is moist.

Sow seeds during early spring under glass, in a temperature of 16°C (60°F). Use a soil-based growing medium. Prick off seedlings into boxes or trays, harden off in the usual way and plant out in late spring, 23cm (9in) apart. Alternatively, broadcast the seeds where they are to flower and thin out later.

Take care

Keep plants moist. 143▸

Viola wittrockiana

(Pansy)

- **Sow in early spring and summer**
- **Well-cultivated soil**
- **Sun or partial shade**

Pansies are hardy, and will flower in sun or partial shade. Many large-flowered F1 and F2 hybrids have recently been introduced. There are several strains able to flower during winter and early spring.

For summer and autumn flowering, seed may be sown in gentle heat under glass in late winter or early spring, or under cold glass in spring. The seedlings should be pricked out and grown cool ready for planting out when large enough. Summer and autumn sowings can be made in a sheltered position in the open or in cold frames for the following year. Pansies appreciate good fertilized soils enriched with well-rotted compost or manure. Prompt removal of dead flowers will promote continual flowering. Keep watered in dry weather and watch for aphids, which check growth.

Take care
Plant on a fresh site each year to avoid soil diseases. 143▸

Viscaria elegans 'Love'

(Silene coeli-rosa)

- **Sow in autumn or spring**
- **Ordinary soil**
- **Sun or partial shade**

The cultivar 'Love' has lovely rose-carmine flowers that start to flower in early summer. Salver-shaped and 2.5cm (1in) across, the blooms of this hardy annual are carried on very slender stems 25cm (10in) high. Leaves are grey-green and tend to be oblong in shape. Overall, plants have a light appearance. This species of the campion family will tolerate some shade, which makes it useful for the difficult position where colour is required in such a situation. Being medium in height, it is suitable towards the front of an annual or mixed border.

These plants are easily raised from seed. Sow them where they are to flower. Take out shallow drills during autumn or spring, and lightly cover the seed. Thin out seedlings to 15cm (6in) apart when they are large enough to handle. Autumn-sown plants will be stronger and flower slightly earlier.

Take care
Avoid watering overhead in hot sunny weather. 144▸

Zea japonica 'Harlequin Mixed'

(Ornamental maize)

- **Sow in mid- or late spring**
- **Fertile and well-cultivated soil**
- **Sunny position**

This is a form of maize prized in the large annual or mixed border. The 'Harlequin' mixture has a variable pleasing colour range: the large strap-like leaves are striped through the basic green with cream, white, pale pink or rose. Up to 2m (6.5ft) the plants will provide extra height where needed; they give greater impact if planted in groups of three or five, preferably at the back of a border in full sunshine.

Sow seed under glass in spring to produce plants for planting out in early summer. Sow individual seeds into single peat pots of any good growing medium. Keep at a temperature of 16°C (60°F). Harden off carefully and plant out when all risk of frost has passed; space them 45cm (18in) apart. Alternatively, in late spring sow seeds where they are to produce foliage; sow two seeds per station, 45cm (18in) apart, and take out the weaker of the two when germination is complete.

Take care

Water well in the summer

Zinnia elegans 'Chippendale Daisy'

- **Sow in spring**
- **Ordinary well-drained soil**
- **Sunny location**

Zinnias are invaluable for bedding purposes. 'Chippendale Daisy' is a very vivid cultivar: the single flowers have intense dark red centres surrounded by bright yellow petal tips – very striking. Blooms measure up to 5cm (2in) in diameter. Stems carrying these blooms have ovate pointed light green leaves. In height, plants will be no more than 60cm (24in). 'Chippendale Daisy' is ideally suited for most purposes, as long as you can provide a sunny site. On borders, plant towards the centre, near light-coloured flowers of a similar height.

Sow under glass in spring at a temperature of 16°C (60°F). Use any good growing medium. When pricking off, use individual peat pots for each single seedling; this will avoid any major disturbance of the roots or stems at planting-out time. Harden off carefully in the usual way at the end of spring and plant out in early summer, 30cm (12in) apart.

Take care

Do not plant out too early.

Zinnia elegans 'Hobgoblin Mixed'

- **Sow in spring**
- **Ordinary, well-drained soil**
- **Sunny position**

The 'Hobgoblin' mixture has a particularly good range of colour, in shades of red, pink, yellow and gold.

Stem length is about 25cm (10in); they are branched and make good bushy compact plants. Leaves are ovate, pointed and light green. Both stems and leaves are covered with stiff hairs. These plants are ideal for borders and beds in a sunny situation although the 'pumila'-type flowerheads are very weather-resistant, and the rain easily runs off the individual blooms.

As a tender half-hardy annual, this plant will need to be raised from seed under glass in spring. Sow seeds in any good growing medium that is free-draining. Keep at a temperature of 16°C (60°F). Prick out seedlings into individual peat pots; this will avoid handling the stems at a later date, which can be damaging. Grow on in the usual way and harden off at the end of spring. Plant out carefully in early summer, 23cm (9in) apart.

Take care
Avoid overwatering at any stage. 144▸

Zinnia elegans 'Ruffles Hybrids'

- **Sow in spring**
- **Ordinary, well-drained soil**
- **Sunny position**

Another zinnia of great potential, the 'Ruffles Hybrid' gives extra height for the annual border or large formal bed. The stems, 60-75cm (24-30in) tall, carry quite weather-resistant flowers of yellow, cherry, pink, scarlet, orange and white. The stiff ruff-like blooms have water-repellent properties. Long branching stems provide useful cut flowers for the house, but plant good-sized drifts in the middle of a large border, or formal beds for a continuous show of colour throughout the summer.

Sow seeds of this tender half-hardy annual during spring. Keep the greenhouse temperature at a constant 16°C (60°F) while seeds are germinating. Use a peat-based growing medium for sowing and pricking off. Pot the seedlings singly into small pots; in this way, less harm will be caused to them at planting-out time. Harden off in the usual way and plant out carefully in summer, 30cm (12in) apart.

Take care
Do not plant out too early.

Index of Common Names

Credits

Line artwork
The drawings in this book have been prepared by Maureen Holt.

Photographs
The majority of the photographs in this book have been taken by Eric Crichton.

Copyright in the following photographs belongs to the suppliers:
Eric Crichton: 9, 15(B), 36, 38-9(B), 70, 71(B), 73, 80(B), 100(TR), 103(BR), 104(TL), 105(TR, BR), 106-7(T), 110(B), 112, 141.

Ralph Gould: 15(T), 39(T), 44(T), 74(TL), 100(B), 109(T).

Editorial assistance
Copy-editing and proof-reading: Maureen Cartwright.

Left: Brachycome iberidifolia

PRINTED IN BELGIUM BY proost INTERNATIONAL BOOK PRODUCTION